Level 2

¡Avancemos!

Unit 3 Resource Book

HOLT McDOUGAL
a division of Houghton Mifflin Harcourt

Fine Art Acknowledgments

Page 87 *El Gobernador don Miguel Antonio de Ustáriz* (1792), José Campeche. Oil on wood. Instituto de Cultura Puertorriqueña, San Juan, Puerto Rico.

Page 88 *Bisonte con palmeras (Bison with Palm Trees) (ca. 1825–1850)*, Goyena Family. Watercolor on ivory, 2 3/8 x 2 in. (6.1 x 5.2 cm). Teodoro Vidal Collection (1996.91.16), Smithsonian American Art Museum, Washington, DC/Art Resource, NY.

Page 89 *La fiesta del vejigante* (2005), Obed Gómez. Acrylic on canvas, 30″ x 40″. Courtesy of the artist.

Page 90 *Descenso del paraíso* (2002), Edward Ferraioli. Mosaico en cristal sobre madera, 39″ x 96″. Courtesy of Instituto de Cultura Puertorriqueña, San Juan, Puerto Rico.

ISBN-13: 978-0-618-75357-4
ISBN-10: 0-618-75357-5   3 4 5 6 7 8 9 1421 12 11 10 09
Internet: www.holtmcdougal.com

HOLT McDOUGAL

¡Avancemos!

Table of Contents

To the Teacher .... vi–xii

Tips for Students .... xiii–xv

DID YOU GET IT? RETEACHING AND PRACTICE COPYMASTERS

Lección 1 1–11

Lección 2 12–22

Answer Key 23–28

PRACTICE GAMES

Lección 1 30–37

Lección 2 38–45

Answer Key 46–49

VIDEO ACTIVITIES COPYMASTERS

Lección 1 50–57

Lección 2 58–65

Answer Key 66–67

VIDEO SCRIPTS

Lección 1 68–69

Lección 2 70–71

AUDIO SCRIPTS

Lección 1 73–77

Lección 2 78–83

MAP/CULTURE ACTIVITIES 84–85

Answer Key 86

FINE ART ACTIVITIES

Lección 1 87–88

Lección 2 89–90

Answer Key 91

FAMILY LETTER 92

FAMILY INVOLVEMENT ACTIVITY 93

ABSENT STUDENT COPYMASTERS

Lección 1 94–101

Lección 2 102–112

To the Teacher

Welcome to *¡Avancemos!* This exciting new Spanish program from McDougal Littell has been designed to provide you—the teacher of today's foreign language classroom—with comprehensive pedagogical support.

PRACTICE WITH A PURPOSE

Activities throughout the program begin by establishing clear goals. Look for the **¡Avanza!** arrow that uses student-friendly language to lead the way towards achievable goals. Built-in self-checks in the student text (**Para y piensa:** Did you get it?) offer the chance to assess student progress throughout the lesson. Both the student text and the workbooks offer abundant leveled practice to match varied student needs.

CULTURE AS A CORNERSTONE

¡Avancemos! celebrates the cultural diversity of the Spanish-speaking world by motivating students to think about similarities and contrasts among different Spanish-speaking cultures. Essential questions encourage thoughtful discussion and comparison between different cultures.

LANGUAGE LEARNING THAT LASTS

The program presents topics in manageable chunks that students will be able to retain and recall. "Recycle" topics are presented frequently so students don't forget material from previous lessons. Previously learned content is built upon and reinforced across the different levels of the program.

TIME-SAVING TEACHER TOOLS

Simplify your planning with McDougal Littell's exclusive teacher resources: the all-inclusive EasyPlanner DVD-ROM, ready-made Power Presentations, and the McDougal Littell Assessment System.

Unit Resource Book

Each Unit Resource Book supports a unit of *¡Avancemos!* The Unit Resource Books provide a wide variety of materials to support, practice, and expand on the material in the *¡Avancemos!* student text.

Components **Following is a list of components included in each Unit Resource Book:**

BACK TO SCHOOL RESOURCES (UNIT 1 ONLY)

Review and start-up activities to support the **Lección preliminar** of the textbook.

DID YOU GET IT? RETEACHING & PRACTICE COPYMASTERS

If students' performance on the **Para y piensa** self-check for a section does not meet your expectations, consider assigning the corresponding Did You Get It? Reteaching and Practice Copymasters. These copymasters provide extensive reteaching and additional practice for every vocabulary and grammar presentation section in *¡Avancemos!* Each vocabulary and grammar section has a corresponding three-page copymaster. The first page of the copymaster reteaches the subject material in a fresh manner. Immediately following this presentation page are two pages of practice exercises that help the student master the topic. The practice pages have engaging contexts and structures to retain students' attention.

PRACTICE GAMES

These games provide fun practice of the vocabulary and grammar just taught. They are targeted in scope so that each game practices a specific area of the **lesson**: *Práctica de vocabulario, Vocabulario en contexto, Práctica de gramática, Gramática en contexto, Todo junto, Repaso de la lección*, and the lesson's cultural information.

Video and audio resources

VIDEO ACTIVITIES

These two-page copymasters accompany the Vocabulary Video and each scene of the **Telehistoria** in Levels 1 and 2 and the **Gran desafío** in Level 3. The pre-viewing activity asks students to activate prior knowledge about a theme or subject related to the scene they will watch. The viewing activity is a simple activity for students to complete as they watch the video. The post-viewing activity gives students the opportunity to demonstrate comprehension of the video episode.

VIDEO SCRIPTS

This section provides the scripts of each video feature in the unit.

AUDIO SCRIPTS

This section contains scripts for all presentations and activities that have accompanying audio in the student text as well as in the two workbooks (*Cuaderno: práctica por niveles* and *Cuaderno para hispanohablantes*) and the assessment program.

Culture resources

MAP/CULTURE ACTIVITIES

This section contains a copymaster with geography and culture activities based on the Unit Opener in the textbook.

FINE ART ACTIVITIES

The fine art activities in every lesson ask students to analyze pieces of art that have been selected as representative of the unit location country. These copymasters can be used in conjunction with the full-color fine art transparencies in the Unit Transparency Book.

Home-school connection

FAMILY LETTERS & FAMILY INVOLVEMENT ACTIVITIES

This section is designed to help increase family support of the students' study of Spanish. The family letter keeps families abreast of the class's progress, while the family involvement activities let students share their Spanish language skills with their families in the context of a game or fun activity.

ABSENT STUDENT COPYMASTERS

The Absent Student Copymasters enable students who miss part of a **lesson** to go over the material on their own. The checkbox format allows teachers to choose and indicate exactly what material the student should complete. The Absent Student Copymasters also offer strategies and techniques to help students understand new or challenging information.

Core Ancillaries in the ¡Avancemos! Program

Leveled workbooks

CUADERNO: PRÁCTICA POR NIVELES

This core ancillary is a leveled practice workbook to supplement the student text. It is designed for use in the classroom or as homework. Students who can complete the activities correctly should be able to pass the quizzes and tests. Practice is organized into three levels of difficulty, labeled A, B, and C. Level B activities are designed to practice vocabulary, grammar, and other core concepts at a level appropriate to most of your students. Students who require more structure can complete Level A activities, while students needing more of a challenge should be encouraged to complete the activities in Level C. Each level provides a different degree of linguistic support, yet requires students to know and handle the same vocabulary and grammar content.

The following sections are included in *Cuaderno: práctica por niveles* for each **lesson**:

Vocabulario A, B, C	Escuchar A, B, C
Gramática 1 A, B, C	Leer A, B, C
Gramática 2 A, B, C	Escribir A, B, C
Integración: Hablar	Cultura A, B, C
Integración: Escribir	

CUADERNO PARA HISPANOHABLANTES

This core ancillary provides leveled practice for heritage learners of Spanish. Level A is for heritage learners who hear Spanish at home but who may speak little Spanish themselves. Level B is for those who speak some Spanish but don't read or write it yet and who may lack formal education in Spanish. Level C is for heritage learners who have had some formal schooling in Spanish. These learners can read and speak Spanish, but may need further development of their writing skills. The *Cuaderno para hispanohablantes* will ensure that heritage learners practice the same basic grammar, reading, and writing skills taught in the student text. At the same time, it offers additional instruction and challenging practice designed specifically for students with prior knowledge of Spanish.

The following sections are included in *Cuaderno para hispanohablantes* for each **lesson**:

Vocabulario A, B, C	Integración: Hablar
Vocabulario adicional	Integración: Escribir
Gramática 1 A, B, C	Lectura A, B, C
Gramática 2 A, B, C	Escritura A, B, C
Gramática adicional	Cultura A, B, C

Other Ancillaries

ASSESSMENT PROGRAM

For each level of *¡Avancemos!*, there are four complete assessment options. Every option assesses students' ability to use the lesson and unit vocabulary and grammar, as well as assessing reading, writing, listening, speaking, and cultural knowledge. The on-level tests are designed to assess the language skills of most of your students. Modified tests provide more support, explanation and scaffolding to enable students with learning difficulties to produce language at the same level as their peers. Pre-AP* tests build the test-taking skills essential to success on Advanced Placement tests. The assessments for heritage learners are all in Spanish, and take into account the strengths that native speakers bring to language learning.

In addition to leveled lesson and unit tests, there is a complete array of vocabulary, culture, and grammar quizzes. All tests include scoring rubrics and point teachers to specific resources for remediation.

UNIT TRANSPARENCY BOOKS—1 PER UNIT

Each transparency book includes:

- Map Atlas Transparencies (Unit 1 only)
- Unit Opener Map Transparencies
- Fine Art Transparencies
- Vocabulary Transparencies
- Grammar Presentation Transparencies
- Situational Transparencies with Label Overlay (plus student copymasters)
- Warm Up Transparencies
- Student Book and Workbook Answer Transparencies

LECTURAS PARA TODOS

A workbook-style reader, *Lecturas para todos*, offers all the readings from the student text as well as additional literary readings in an interactive format. In addition to the readings, they contain reading strategies, comprehension questions, and tools for developing vocabulary.

There are four sections in each *Lecturas para todos*:

- *¡Avancemos!* readings with annotated skill-building support
- *Literatura adicional*—additional literary readings
- Academic and Informational Reading Development
- Test Preparation Strategies

* AP and the Advanced Placement Program are registered trademarks of the College Entrance Examination Board, which was not involved in the production of and does not endorse this product.

LECTURAS PARA HISPANOHABLANTES

Lecturas para hispanohablantes offers additional cultural readings for heritage learners and a rich selection of literary readings. All readings supported by reading strategies, comprehension questions, tools for developing vocabulary, plus tools for literary analysis.

There are four sections in each *Lecturas para hispanohablantes*:

- *En voces* cultural readings with annotated skill-building support

- *Literatura adicional*—high-interest readings by prominent authors from around the Spanish-speaking world. Selections were chosen carefully to reflect the diversity of experiences Spanish-speakers bring to the classroom.

- Bilingual Academic and Informational Reading Development

- Bilingual Test Preparation Strategies, for success on standardized tests in English

COMIC BOOKS

These fun, motivating comic books are written in a contemporary, youthful style with full-color illustrations. Each comic uses the target language students are learning. There is one 32-page comic book for each level of the program.

TPRS: TEACHING PROFICIENCY THROUGH READING AND STORYTELLING

This book includes an up-to-date guide to TPRS and TPRS stories written by Piedad Gutiérrez that use *¡Avancemos!* lesson-specific vocabulary.

MIDDLE SCHOOL RESOURCE BOOK

- Practice activities to support the 1b Bridge lesson

- Diagnostic and Bridge Unit Tests

- Transparencies
  - Vocabulary Transparencies
  - Grammar Transparencies
  - Answer Transparencies for the Student Text
  - Bridge Warm Up Transparencies

- Audio CDs

LESSON PLANS

- Lesson Plans with suggestions for modifying instruction
- Core and Expansion options clearly noted
- IEP suggested modifications
- Substitute teacher lesson plans

BEST PRACTICES TOOLKIT

Strategies for Effective Teaching

- Research-based Learning Strategies
- Language Learning that Lasts: Teaching for Long-term Retention
- Culture as a Cornerstone/Cultural Comparisons
- English Grammar Connection
- Building Vocabulary
- Developing Reading Skills
- Differentiation
- Best Practices in Teaching Heritage Learners
- Assessment (including Portfolio Assessment, Reteaching and Remediation)
- Best Practices Swap Shop: Favorite Activities for Teaching Reading, Writing, Listening, Speaking
- Reading, Writing, Listening, and Speaking Strategies in the World Languages classroom
- ACTFL Professional Development Articles
- Thematic Teaching
- Best Practices in Middle School

Using Technology in the World Languages Classroom

Tools for Motivation

- Games in the World Languages Classroom
- Teaching Proficiency through Reading and Storytelling
- Using Comic Books for Motivation

Pre-AP and International Baccalaureate

- International Baccalaureate
- Pre-AP

Graphic Organizer Transparencies

- Teaching for Long-term Retention
- Teaching Culture
- Building Vocabulary
- Developing Reading Skills

Absent Student Copymasters—Tips for Students

LISTENING TO CDS AT HOME

- Open your text, workbook, or class notes to the corresponding pages that relate to the audio you will listen to. Read the assignment directions if there are any. Do these steps before listening to the audio selections.

- Listen to the CD in a quiet place. Play the CD loudly enough so that you can hear everything clearly. Keep focused. Play a section several times until you understand it. Listen carefully. Repeat aloud with the CD. Try to sound like the people on the CD. Stop the CD when you need to do so.

- If you are lost, stop the CD. Replay it and look at your notes. Take a break if you are not focusing. Return and continue after a break. Work in short periods of time: 5 or 10 minutes at a time so that you remain focused and energized.

QUESTION/ANSWER SELECTIONS

- If there is a question/answer selection, read the question aloud several times. Write down the question. Highlight the key words, verb endings, and any new words. Look up new words and write their meaning. Then say everything aloud.

- One useful strategy for figuring out questions is to put parentheses around groups of words that go together. For example: **(¿Cuántos niños)(van)(al estadio)(a las tres?)** Read each group of words one at a time. Check for meaning. Write out answers. Highlight key words and verb endings. Say the question aloud. Read the answer aloud. Ask yourself if you wrote what you meant.

- Be sure to say everything aloud several times before moving on to the next question. Check for spelling, verb endings, and accent marks.

FLASHCARDS FOR VOCABULARY

- If you have Internet access, go to ClassZone at classzone.com. All the vocabulary taught in *¡Avancemos!* is available on electronic flashcards. Look for the flashcards in the *¡Avancemos!* section of ClassZone.

- If you don't have Internet access, write the Spanish word or phrase on one side of a 3″ × 5″ card, and the English translation on the other side. Illustrate your flashcards when possible. Be sure to highlight any verb endings, accent marks, or other special spellings that will need a bit of extra attention.

GRAMMAR ACTIVITIES

- Underline or highlight all verb endings and adjective agreements. For example:
Nosotros comemos pollo rico.

- Underline or highlight infinitive endings: **trabajar**.

- Underline or highlight accented letters. Say aloud and be louder on the accented letters. Listen carefully for the loudness. This will remind you where to write your accent mark. For example: **lápiz**, **lápices**, **árbol**, **árboles**

- When writing a sentence, be sure to ask yourself, "What do I mean? What am I trying to say?" Then check your sentence to be sure that you wrote what you wanted to say.

- Mark patterns with a highlighter. For example, for stem-changing verbs, you can draw a "boot" around the letters that change:

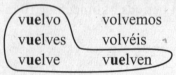

READING AND CULTURE SECTIONS

- Read the strategy box. Copy the graphic organizer so you can fill it out as you read.

- Look at the title and subtitles before you begin to read. Then look at and study any photos and read the captions. Translate the captions only if you can't understand them at all. Before you begin to read, guess what the selection will be about. What do you think that you will learn? What do you already know about this topic?

- Read any comprehension questions before beginning to read the paragraphs. This will help you focus on the upcoming reading selection. Copy the questions and highlight key words.

- Reread one or two of the questions and then go to the text. Begin to read the selection carefully. Read it again. On a sticky note, write down the appropriate question number next to where the answer lies in the text. This will help you keep track of what the questions have asked you and will help you focus when you go back to reread it later, perhaps in preparation for a quiz or test.

- Highlight any new words. Make a list or flashcards of new words. Look up their meanings. Study them. Quiz yourself or have a partner quiz you. Then go back to the comprehension questions and check your answers from memory. Look back at the text if you need to verify your answers.

PAIRED PRACTICE EXERCISES

- If there is an exercise for partners, practice both parts at home.

- If no partner is available, write out both scripts and practice both roles aloud. Highlight and underline key words, verb endings, and accent marks.

WRITING PROJECTS

- Brainstorm ideas before writing.

- Make lists of your ideas.

- Put numbers next to the ideas to determine the order in which you want to write about them.

- Group your ideas into paragraphs.

- Skip lines in your rough draft.

- Have a partner read your work and give you feedback on the meaning and language structure.

- Set it aside and reread it at least once before doing a final draft. Double-check verb endings, adjective agreements, and accents.

- Read it once again to check that you said what you meant to say.

- Be sure to have a title and any necessary illustrations or bibliography.

Did You Get It? *Presentación de vocabulario*

Level 2 pp. 144–145

> ¡AVANZA! **Goal:** Talk about clothes and shopping. Say where you shop and express opinions.

Clothing

• Study the words that are used to talk about clothing and the way they fit.

Clothes	**vestirse** *(to get dressed)*
	las botas *(boots)*
	las sandalias *(sandals)*
	el suéter *(sweater)*
	la pulsera *(bracelet)*
	el traje *(suit)*
	la falda *(skirt)*
	la talla *(clothing size)*
	el cinturón *(belt)*
	el reloj *(watch)*
	de cuadros *(plaid)*
	de rayas *(striped)*
Places to shop	**la joyería** *(jewelry store)*
	la farmacia *(pharmacy)*
	Internet *(Internet)*
	la zapatería *(shoe store)*
	la librería *(bookstore)*
	la panadería *(bakery)*

• Read the following conversation to learn some words and expressions you can use to talk about clothes.

—¿**Cómo me queda** esta falda? *(How does this skirt fit me?)* ¡**Me encanta**! *(I love it!)*

—**En mi opinión** *(In my opinion)*, te queda **apretada** *(tight)*. **Es mala idea** *(It's a bad idea)* comprarla.

—¿Estos jeans me quedan bien o **flojos** *(loose)*?

—Te quedan bien. **Es buena idea** comprarlos. *(It's a good idea . . .)*

—**Creo que sí.** *(I think so.)*

—¿**Podrías recomendarme** una zapatería? *(Could you recommend to me . . .)*

—La Zapatería González es buena. Allí venden zapatos que **están de moda** *(are fashionable)*.

—¿**Está abierta ahora?** *(Is it open now?)*

—**No, ahora está cerrada.** *(No, it's closed now.)*

Did You Get It? *Práctica de vocabulario*

> **¡AVANZA!** **Goal:** Talk about clothes and shopping. Say where you shop and express opinions.

① Write the word for the item shown in each picture.

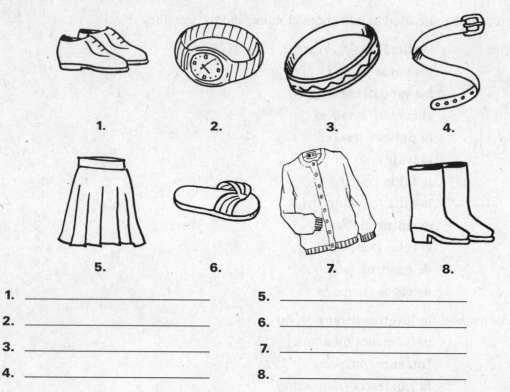

1. 2. 3. 4.

5. 6. 7. 8.

1. _____   5. _____

2. _____   6. _____

3. _____   7. _____

4. _____   8. _____

② Where do you go to buy the following?

1. los zapatos: la panadería   la zapatería   la farmacia

2. una pulsera: la farmacia   la joyería   la librería

3. el pan: la panadería   la farmacia   la zapatería

4. un libro: la zapatería   la joyería   la librería

5. la medicina: la librería   la farmacia   la panadería

③ Where is everyone? Follow the model.

Modelo: Alisa está comprando champú.   *Ella está en la farmacia.*

1. Tomás está comprando botas. _____

2. Las chicas están comprando joyas. _____

3. Tú estás comprando (el) pan. _____

4. Arturo y yo estamos comprando libros. _____

5. Yo estoy comprando un reloj. _____

4 Choose the best expression to describe how everything fits based on the description.

1. La pulsera es muy grande.
   a. Le queda bien.
   b. Le queda floja.

2. Las botas son el número correcto.
   a. Le quedan bien.
   b. Le quedan apretadas.

3. La pulsera es muy grande.
   a. Le queda bien.
   b. Le queda mal.

4. El suéter no es grande ni es pequeño.
   a. Le queda apretado.
   b. Le queda bien.

5. El traje es la talla correcta.
   a. Le queda bien.
   b. Le queda flojo.

6. Los zapatos son pequeños.
   a. Le quedan apretados.
   b. Le quedan flojos.

5 Choose the correct word or phrase to complete the conversation.

de moda	recomiendas	buena idea	apretada
opinión	creo	queda bien	me parece que

Alma: ¿Es _____ ir de compras hoy?

Migdalia: ¡_____ que sí!

Alma: A mí me gusta vestirme con la ropa que está _____ .

Migdalia: A mí también. Pero en mi _____ es mala idea vestirte con ropa de moda si no te _____ .

Alma: Bueno, ¿cómo me queda esta falda negra?

Migdalia: _____ es demasiado pequeña.

Alma: Es verdad. Me queda un poco _____ . ¿Y esta falda marrón?

Migdalia: Esa falda te queda bien.

Alma: ¿Y ésta verde?

Migdalia: También te queda bien.

Alma: ¿Cuál me _____ , la falda marrón o la falda verde?

Migdalia: Las dos. ¡Compra las dos!

6 Answer the following questions in complete sentences in Spanish.

1. ¿Dónde compras botas? _____

2. ¿Qué número de zapatos necesitas? _____

3. ¿Te gusta vestirte con ropa que está de moda? _____

4. ¿Cómo te queda tu ropa favorita? _____

Did You Get It? *Presentación de gramática*

Level 2 p. 149

> **¡AVANZA!** **Goal:** Learn about the irregular **yo** forms of some present-tense verbs.

Irregular *yo* Verbs

• Study the conjugation of the following verbs.

	hacer *(to do/to make)*	poner *(to put)*	salir *(to go out/to leave)*	traer *(to bring)*
yo	ha**go**	pon**go**	sal**go**	tra**igo**
tú	haces	pones	sales	traes

EXPLANATION: The verbs **hacer**, **poner**, **salir**, and **traer** end in **-go** in the **yo** form. Compare them with their **tú** forms in the present tense.

• Now study the conjugation of these verbs.

	decir *(to say)*	venir *(to come)*	tener *(to have)*
yo	di**go**	ven**go**	ten**go**
tú	di**c**es	v**i**enes	t**i**enes

EXPLANATION: The verbs **decir**, **venir**, and **tener** also end in **-go** in the **yo** form. All are stem-changing verbs, but only **decir** changes the stem vowel in the **yo** form.

• Finally, study the conjugation of these verbs.

	conocer *(to know/to meet)*	dar *(to give)*	saber *(to know)*	ver *(to see)*
yo	cono**zco**	d**oy**	s**é**	ve**o**
tú	conoces	das	sabes	ves

EXPLANATION: **Conocer**, **dar**, **saber**, and **ver** also have irregular **yo** forms in the present tense.

Did You Get It? *Práctica de gramática*

> **¡AVANZA!**   **Goal:** Learn about the irregular **yo** forms of some present-tense verbs.

1 Write the correct **yo** form of each verb.

1. tener _____
2. ver _____
3. saber _____
4. traer _____
5. poner _____
6. hacer _____

7. decir _____
8. conocer _____
9. venir _____
10. dar _____
11. salir _____

2 Complete each sentence with the correct form of the verb in parentheses.

1. Yo no _____ clases esta semana. **(tener)**
2. Siempre me _____ zapatos cómodos. **(poner)**
3. Tú también _____ francés. **(saber)**
4. Yo _____ todas las librerías. **(conocer)**
5. ¿Tú _____ que es buena idea? **(decir)**
6. Yo _____ las sandalias a la playa. **(traer)**
7. Yo te _____ un regalo. **(dar)**
8. ¿ _____ tú la tarea? **(hacer)**
9. Yo _____ con mis amigos. **(salir)**
10. ¿ _____ tú ese programa de televisión? **(ver)**

3 Answer yes to the following questions. Follow the model.

Modelo: ¿Tienes que comprar un traje? *Sí, tengo que comprar un traje.*

1. ¿Siempre vienes a este café? _____
2. ¿Siempre dices la verdad? _____
3. ¿Pones la mesa para la cena? _____
4. ¿Conoces a los estudiantes? _____
5. ¿Haces compras por Internet? _____
6. ¿Sales con tus amigos hoy? _____
7. ¿Traes el pastel a la fiesta? _____
8. ¿Le das un regalo a tu amiga? _____
9. ¿Ves todas las películas nuevas? _____

4 Answer the questions in complete sentences based on your own experience.

1. ¿Vienes tarde a la escuela?

_____

2. ¿Haces la cama antes de salir de casa?

_____

3. ¿Sales con tus amigos después de clases?

_____

4. ¿Le das un regalo a tu amigo para su cumpleaños?

_____

5. ¿Conoces tiendas donde venden ropa que está de moda?

_____

6. ¿Les dices siempre la verdad a tus padres?

_____

7. ¿Te pones el uniforme para jugar al béisbol?

_____

8. ¿Sabes todos los secretos de tu mejor amigo(a)?

_____

5 Translate the following.

1. I buy things on the Internet.

_____

2. I have a new skirt.

_____

3. I put the skirt on before putting the blouse on.

_____

4. I give gifts to my friends.

_____

5. I bring my books to class.

_____

6. I watch funny movies.

_____

Did You Get It? *Presentación de gramática*

> **¡AVANZA!**   **Goal:**   Learn the pronouns that follow prepositions.

Pronouns After Prepositions

• Read the following sentences, paying attention to the boldfaced words.

La pulsera es **para mí**. *(The bracelet is **for me**.)*

La zapatería está **delante de ti**. *(The shoe store is **in front of you**.)*

Las botas están **junto a él**. *(The boots are **next to him**.)*

Tenemos las compras **con nosotros**. *(We have the purchases **with us**.)*

La casa está **lejos de ustedes**. *(The house is **far from you**.)*

Los regalos son **para usted**. *(The gifts are **for you**.)*

EXPLANATION: Pronouns that follow prepositions are different from subject pronouns and object pronouns. You can use the pronouns listed above after prepositions such as **para, de, a,** and **con.**

• Read these sentences, paying attention to the boldfaced words.

¿Vas **conmigo** a la zapatería? *(Are you going **with me** to the shoe store?)*

Sí, voy **contigo**. *(Yes, I'm going **with you**.)*

EXPLANATION: When you use **mí** and **ti** after the preposition **con**, they form the words **conmigo** and **contigo.**

• Read the following sentences, paying attention to the highlighted words.

A mí no me gusta comprar por Internet.   *(I don't like buying on the Internet.)*

A él no le gusta la ropa de cuadros.   *(He doesn't like plaid clothes.)*

EXPLANATION: With verbs like **gustar**, you can use pronouns after **a** to add emphasis.

• Read these sentences, paying attention to the boldfaced words.

No le gusta la ropa apretada.   *(He/she/you don't like tight clothes.)*

A ella no le gusta la ropa apretada.   *(**She** doesn't like tight clothes.)*

Le regalaron un traje marrón.   *(They gave him/her/you a brown suit as a gift.)*

A él le regalaron un traje marrón.   *(They gave **him** a brown suit as a gift.)*

EXPLANATION: The pronoun after **a** also can clarify to whom the sentence refers.

Did You Get It? *Práctica de gramática*

UNIDAD 3 Lección 1

Reteaching and Practice

¡AVANZA!	**Goal:** Learn the pronouns that follow prepositions.

1 Complete the sentences.

nosotros	él	ella	mí	ellas	ti

1. Es de _____ . *(It's hers.)*

2. Está al lado de _____ . *(It's beside you.)*

3. La ropa es de _____ . *(The clothes are his.)*

4. Quiero ir con _____ . *(I want to go with them.)*

5. Los niños están con _____ . *(The children are with us.)*

6. La pulsera es para _____ . *(The bracelet is for me.)*

2 Write each tag in Spanish.

1.   2.   3.   4.   5.

1. Para _____

2. Para _____

3. Para _____

4. Para _____

5. Para _____

3 Complete the translations clarifying to whom each sentence refers. Follow the model.

Modelo: She likes jewelry.

    <u>A ella</u> le gustan las joyas.

1. *I like to go to the bookstore.* _____ me gusta ir a la librería.

2. *Do you like the suit?* ¿_____ te gusta el traje?

3. *We like music.* _____ nos gusta la música.

4. *They don't like to go shopping.* _____ no les gusta ir de compras.

5. *He likes all the boots.* _____ le gustan todas las botas.

4 Answer the following questions, using one of these verbs in your answer: **gustar**, **encantar**, **importar**, and **interesar**. Follow the model.

Modelo: —¿A ti te gusta hacer compras en la zapatería?

—*Sí, a mí me encanta hacer compras en la zapatería.*

1. ¿A ti te gusta comprar por Internet?

_____

2. ¿A ti te gusta la ropa que está de moda?

_____

3. ¿A ti te gustan los trajes apretados?

_____

4. ¿A ti te gusta ir a la librería?

_____

5. ¿A ti te gusta la clase de español?

_____

5 Translate the following sentences.

1. My mother is going shopping with me.

_____

2. We want to buy these boots for you.

_____

3. You don't like this skirt.

_____

4. José, can I go with you?

_____

5. The jewelry store is in front of us!

_____

6. I really love the bracelet!

_____

¿Recuerdas?

Expressions of frequency

- Study the following expressions of frequency in Spanish.

> **siempre** *(always)*
>
> **nunca** *(never)*
>
> **todos los días** *(every day)*
>
> **de vez en cuando** *(once in a while)*

Práctica

1 Choose the most logical response to each statement.

1. A Pedro no le gusta hacer ejercicio.

   a. Va al gimnasio todos los días.　　**b.** Nunca va al gimnasio.

2. A Lola le encantan las joyas.

   a. Nunca va a la joyería.　　**b.** Siempre va a la joyería.

3. A mí me gusta comprar zapatos.

   a. Voy a la zapatería de vez en cuando.　　**b.** Nunca voy a la zapatería.

4. A ti no te interesa la ropa que está de moda.

   a. Nunca compras ropa nueva.　　**b.** Siempre compras ropa nueva.

5. A mí me molesta llevar una gorra.

   a. Llevo un gorro sólo de vez en cuando.　　**b.** Siempre llevo un gorro.

2 Tell how often you do the following. Use **siempre**, **nunca**, **todos los días**, or **de vez en cuando**.

1. dar fiestas _____

2. ir a la biblioteca _____

3. comprar por Internet _____

4. ver películas de horror _____

5. estudiar español _____

6. comprar ropa _____

7. leer novelas _____

8. hacer la tarea _____

9. escribir poesía _____

10. sacar buenas notas _____

¿Recuerdas?

Clothes

- Study the following words we use to talk about clothes.

Clothes	**el gorro** *(winter hat)*
	el sombrero *(hat)*
	la ropa *(clothing)*
	la camisa *(shirt)*
	la camiseta *(T-shirt)*
	la chaqueta *(jacket)*
	los jeans *(jeans)*
	los pantalones *(pants)*
	los pantalones cortos *(shorts)*
	las botas *(boots)*
Putting on clothes	**ponerse la ropa** *(to put clothes on)*
	vestirse *(to get dressed)*

Práctica

What do they wear and when? Form sentences with the words given. Follow the model.

Modelo: Elena / ponerse pantalones cortos / cuando hace calor
Ella se pone pantalones cortos cuando hace calor.

1. yo / ponerse una camiseta / en el verano

    _____

2. ellos / ponerse los jeans / cuando hace frío

    _____

3. Alejandro y yo / ponerse un sombrero / cuando hace sol

    _____

4. tú / ponerse una chaqueta / cuando hace viento

    _____

5. Luis y Javier / ponerse las botas / cuando nieva

    _____

6. ustedes / ponerse los pantalones cortos / cuando hace mucho sol

    _____

UNIDAD 3 Lección 1   Reteaching and Practice

UNIDAD 3 Lección 2

Reteaching and Practice

Did You Get It? *Presentación de vocabulario*

> **¡AVANZA!** **Goal:** Talk about items at a marketplace, and learn to use polite expressions.

Items at a Marketplace

- Below is a list of words used to describe items you might find at a marketplace. Study the words.

Items	**el retrato** *(portrait)*
	la pintura *(painting)*
	la escultura *(sculpture)*
	los artículos *(goods)*
	una ganga *(a bargain)*
	los artículos *(goods)*
Descriptions	**hecho(s) a mano** *(hand-made)*
	de plata *(of silver)*
	de cuero *(of leather)*
	de oro *(of gold)*
	de metal *(of metal)*
	de cerámica *(of ceramic)*
	de madera *(of wood)*
	de piedra *(of stone)*
	fino(a) *(fine)*
	único(a) *(unique)*
	barato(a) *(inexpensive)*

Expressions of Courtesy

- Read the ways to address people politely.

Gracias. *(Thank you.)*
De nada. *(You're welcome.)*

Con permiso. *(Excuse me.)*
Pase. *(Go ahead.)*

Perdóneme. *(I'm sorry.)*
Disculpe. *(Excuse me. / I'm sorry . . .)*
¿Puedo ver... ? ¿Podría mostrarme... ? ¿Me deja ver... ? *(May I see . . . ?)*
Con mucho gusto. *(With pleasure.)*

Did You Get It? *Práctica de vocabulario*

| ¡AVANZA! | **Goal:** Talk about items at a marketplace, and learn to use polite expressions. |

1 What is . . . ?

1. a good purchase at a cheap price?

   una escultura   una ganga   un retrato

2. a painting of a person?

   un retrato   una escultura   un artículo

3. a unique sculpture?

   una escultura barata   una escultura fina   una escultura única

4. an article made by hand?

   un artículo hecho a mano   un artículo caro   un artículo barato

5. an article made out of gold?

   un artículo hecho a mano   un artículo de oro   un artículo de plata

6. a painting?

   un artículo   una pintura   una escultura

2 Write the most logical choice to complete each dialogue. Use each expression from the box only once.

Sí, son muy finas. Con mucho gusto.	Es de metal. Pase, por favor.	¿Puedo entrar? De nada.

1. —¿ Puedo ver esa escultura?

   —_____

2. —¿De qué es la escultura?

   —_____

3. —Nos gustaría ver el retrato.

   —_____

4. —_____

   —Sí, pase.

5. —Las joyas son muy originales.

   —_____

6. —Gracias.

   —_____

3 Complete the following translations.

1. a gold necklace   un collar _____
2. a fine bracelet   una pulsera _____
3. a unique sculpture   una escultura _____
4. a hand-made hat   un sombrero _____
5. a silver ring   un anillo _____
6. inexpensive shoes   unos zapatos _____
7. What a bargain!   ¡Qué _____ !
8. a stone sculpture   una escultura _____
9. a beautiful portrait un _____ bello.
10. wooden goods   los artículos _____

4 Imagine that you are at an open-air market. What do you say if . . . ?

1. you want to see a painting?

_____

2. you want to see a stone sculpture?

_____

3. you want to know if a bracelet is made of gold?

_____

4. you want to say "you're welcome"?

_____

5. you bump into someone?

_____

6. you want to tell the vendor that you are looking for inexpensive items?

_____

5 Write a complete sentence describing two things you bought recently at a market and what each was made of.

_____

_____

Did You Get It? *Presentación de gramática*

> **¡AVANZA!**   **Goal:**   Learn five verbs with irregular preterite stems.

Irregular Verbs in the Preterite

• Study the following verbs, stems, and preterite endings.

Verb	Stem	Preterite Endings	
estar *(to be)*	estuv-	-e	-imos
poder *(to be able)*	pud-	-iste	-isteis
poner *(to put)*	pus-	-o	-ieron
saber *(to know)*	sup-		
tener *(to have)*	tuv-		

EXPLANATION: The Spanish verbs **estar**, **poder**, **poner**, **saber** and **tener** are irregular in the preterite tense. To form the preterite of these verbs, you need to change their stems and add irregular preterite endings.

• Read the following sentence, paying attention to the boldfaced verb.

   Yo **supe** la respuesta esta mañana.   *(I **found out** the answer this morning.)*

EXPLANATION: The verb **saber** has a different meaning in the preterite. It means *to find out*.

Did You Get It? *Práctica de gramática*

¡AVANZA!	**Goal:** Learn five verbs with irregular preterite stems.

❶ Write the correct form of the following verbs in the preterite.

1. estar   yo _____

ustedes / ellos _____

tú _____

Ariana y yo _____

usted _____

2. tener   Ana y Luisa _____

nosotros _____

ella _____

tú _____

yo _____

3. poner   usted _____

yo _____

Rodrigo y yo _____

ustedes _____

él _____

4. poder   tú _____

Emiliana _____

los chicos _____

usted _____

nosotras _____

5. tener   Lorenzo y Pablo _____

yo _____

Andrea, Alicia y yo _____

ellas _____

ustedes _____

❷ Write the following in Spanish in the preterite.

1. you *(pl.)* were _____

2. they could _____

3. we found out _____

4. Lorenzo and Lupe put _____

5. Patricia had _____

6. the boys were _____

7. we put _____

8. you *(pl.)* had _____

9. I found out _____

10. you *(familiar, sing.)* could _____

3 Complete the paragraph with the correct form of **estar**, **poder**, **poner**, **saber**, and **tener**.

Ayer Anastasia y yo **1.** _____ en el mercado de artesanías. Nosotros **2.** _____ que en el mercado hay muchas gangas. Vimos muchas cosas bonitas en el mercado. Yo compré unas botas de cuero baratas. Anastasia compró una pulsera bonita. Nosotros no **3.** _____ pagar con tarjeta de crédito. **4.** _____ que pagar con dinero en efectivo. Cuando salimos del mercado yo me **5.** _____ las botas y ella se **6.** _____ la pulsera.

4 Translate the sentences into Spanish.

1. She was here yesterday.

_____

2. They found out the truth last week.

_____

3. We had it last year.

_____

4. Mr. Sánchez put it there yesterday.

_____

5. You finally were able to write the e-mail.

_____

6. I found out now.

_____

7. They were here last week.

_____

8. He had it last month.

_____

9. They were able to go on Tuesday.

_____

10. She finally put on the boots.

_____

Did You Get It? *Presentación de gramática*

¡AVANZA! **Goal:** Understand the preterite forms of **-ir** stem changing verbs.

Preterite Tense of *-ir* Stem Changing Verbs

• Read the conjugation of **pedir** and **dormir** in the preterite.

Preterite tense e ⟶ i		Preterite tense o ⟶ u	
pedir *(to ask for)*		**dormir** *(to sleep)*	
pedí	pedimos	dormí	dormimos
pediste	pedisteis	dormiste	dormisteis
pidió	pidieron	durmió	durmieron

EXPLANATION: Many **-ir** verbs have stem changes in the present tense. These verbs change stems in some forms of the preterite tense, too. Stem-changing **-ir** verbs in the preterite change only in the **usted/él/ella** and the **ustedes/ellos/ellas** forms.

There are other Spanish verbs that follow the pattern of **pedir**. Read the chart below, paying attention to the underlined letters.

seguir *(to follow)*	preferir *(to prefer)*	vestirse *(to get dressed)*	servir *(to serve)*	competir *(to compete)*
seguí	preferí	me vestí	serví	competí
seguiste	preferiste	te vestiste	serviste	competiste
siguió	prefirió	se vistió	sirvió	compitió
seguimos	preferimos	nos vestimos	servimos	competimos
seguisteis	preferisteis	os vestisteis	servisteis	competisteis
siguieron	prefirieron	se vistieron	sirvieron	compitieron

UNIDAD 3 Lección 2

Reteaching and Practice

Did You Get It? *Práctica de gramática*

> **¡AVANZA!**　**Goal:** Understand the preterite forms of **-ir** stem changing verbs.

① Write the correct form of the following verbs in the preterite.

1. **pedir**　yo _____
　　　　　　ellas _____
　　　　　　usted _____

2. **dormir**　Ana y Luisa _____
　　　　　　　nosotros _____
　　　　　　　tú _____

3. **seguir**　tú _____
　　　　　　ustedes _____
　　　　　　él _____

4. **preferir**　tú _____
　　　　　　　Emiliana _____
　　　　　　　las chicas _____

5. **servir**　Lucía y yo _____
　　　　　　Alicia _____
　　　　　　ellos _____

6. **vestirse**　nosotras _____
　　　　　　　los estudiantes _____
　　　　　　　tú _____

② Write the correct preterite form for the verb in parentheses.

1. Carolina _____ un sándwich. **(pedir)**
2. Mi hermano _____ en la maratón. **(competir)**
3. Nosotros _____ toda la mañana. **(dormir)**
4. Ustedes _____ las instrucciones. **(seguir)**
5. El camarero nos _____ la comida. **(servir)**
6. Ustedes _____ el menú. **(pedir)**
7. ¿ _____ ustedes en el campeonato? **(competir)**
8. Nosotros _____ rápido. **(vestirse)**
9. Los chicos _____ hamburguesas. **(pedir)**
10. ¿Qué libro _____ tu hermano? **(prefer)**

UNIDAD 3 Lección 2

Reteaching and Practice

❸ Use the appropriate preterite and present tense forms to complete each set of sentences.

1. dormir

Ayer tú _____ poco.

Hoy tú _____ mucho.

2. competir

La semana pasada ellos _____ en el gimnasio.

Esta semana ellos _____ en el estadio.

3. seguir

El año pasado, tú _____ la moda.

Este año, tú no _____ la moda.

4. pedir

El mes pasado usted _____ un collar de plata.

Ahora, usted _____ un collar de oro.

5. vestirse

Anteayer usted _____ antes de desayunar.

Hoy usted _____ después de desayunar.

❹ Translate the following sentences into Spanish.

1. They ordered pizza.

_____

2. I got dressed early today.

_____

3. You served a good dinner.

_____

4. Emiliana slept eight hours.

_____

5. My friends competed in the championship.

_____

6. She preferred to go to the movies.

_____

7. We followed the lesson.

_____

8. The waiter served a cold soup.

_____

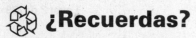 ## ¿Recuerdas?

Family Members and Chores

- You have learned many words to talk about family members. Review these.

La familia *(family)*

la madre (la mamá) *(mother, mom)*	**el padre (el papá)** *(father, dad)*	**los padres** *(parents)*
la hermana *(sister)*	**el hermano** *(brother)*	**los hermanos** *(brothers and sisters)*
la hija *(daughter)*	**el hijo** *(son)*	**los hijos** *(children)*
la abuela *(grandmother)*	**el abuelo** *(grandfather)*	**los abuelos** *(grandparents)*
la tía *(aunt)*	**el tío** *(uncle)*	**los tíos** *(aunts and uncles)*
la prima *(female cousin)*	**el primo** *(male cousin)*	**los primos** *(cousins)*

- You also have learned words about chores. Review these.

Los quehaceres *(chores)*

hacer la cama *(to make the bed)*	**lavar los platos** *(to wash the dishes)*
barrer el suelo *(to sweep the floor)*	**sacar la basura** *(to take out the trash)*
cortar el césped *(to cut the grass)*	**pasar la aspiradora** *(to vacuum)*
poner la mesa *(to set the table)*	**limpiar la cocina** *(to clean the kitchen)*

Práctica

Which family members had to do the following chores? Follow the model.

Modelo: my grandmother / set the table

Mi abuela tuvo que poner la mesa.

1. my mom / sweep the floor

_____

2. my sisters / do the dishes

_____

3. my grandfather / cut the grass

_____

4. my brother and I / clean the kitchen

_____

5. I / take out the garbage

_____

Right margin: **UNIDAD 3 Lección 2   Reteaching and Practice**

♻ ¿Recuerdas?

Foods

• You already have learned words about food. Read and review the list below.

el pescado (fish)	**el arroz** (rice)
el pollo (chicken)	**la ensalada** (salad)
las uvas (grapes)	**la hamburguesa** (hamburger)
la sopa (soup)	**el pan** (bread)
el pastel (cake)	**la pizza** (pizza)
la leche (milk)	**el tomate** (tomato)

Práctica

❶ Match the following.

1. _____ el pescado   **a.** hamburger

2. _____ el pollo   **b.** rice

3. _____ las uvas   **c.** soup

4. _____ la sopa   **d.** fish

5. _____ el pastel   **e.** milk

6. _____ la ensalada   **f.** chicken

7. _____ la hamburguesa   **g.** grapes

8. _____ el pan   **h.** bread

9. _____ la leche   **i.** cake

10. _____ el arroz   **j.** salad

❷ Think about the last time you went to a restaurant. Use the verb **pedir** to write three or four sentences describing what you and others ordered. Follow the model.

Modelo: *La última vez que fui a un restaurante yo pedí una hamburguesa con queso. Mi mamá pidió una ensalada. Mi papá pidió pescado. Mis hermanos pidieron una pizza.*

_____

_____

_____

Did You Get It? Answer Key

PRÁCTICA DE VOCABULARIO
CLOTHES AND SHOPPING, pp. 2–3

❶

1. los zapatos
2. el reloj
3. la pulsera
4. el cinturón
5. la falda
6. la sandalia
7. el suéter
8. las botas

❷

1. la zapatería
2. la joyería
3. la panadería
4. la librería
5. la farmacia

❸

1. Él está en la zapatería.
2. Ellas están en la joyería.
3. Yo estoy (Tú estás) en la panadería.
4. Ustedes están (Nosotros estamos) en la librería.
5. Tú estás (Yo estoy) en la joyería.

❹

1. b
2. a
3. b
4. b
5. a
6. a

❺

buena idea, Creo, de moda, opinión, queda bien, Me parece que, apretada, recomiendas

❻ *Answers may vary.*

1. Compro botas (Las compro) en la zapatería.
2. Necesito el número...
3. Sí, me gusta vestirme con ropa que está de moda.
4. Mi ropa favorita me queda bien.

Did You Get It? Answer Key

PRÁCTICA DE GRAMÁTICA
IRREGULAR *YO* VERBS, pp. 5, 6

①

1. tengo
2. veo
3. sé
4. traigo
5. pongo
6. hago
7. digo
8. conozco
9. vengo
10. doy
11. salgo

②

1. tengo
2. pongo
3. sabes
4. conozco
5. dices
6. traigo
7. doy
8. Haces
9. salgo
10. Ves

③

1. Sí, siempre vengo a este café.
2. Sí, siempre digo la verdad.
3. Sí, pongo la mesa para la cena.
4. Sí, conozco a los estudiantes.
5. Sí, hago compras por Internet.
6. Sí, salgo con mis amigos hoy.
7. Sí, traigo el pastel a la fiesta.
8. Sí, le doy un regalo a mi amiga.
9. Sí, veo todas las películas nuevas.

④

1. Sí, (No, no) vengo tarde a la escuela.
2. Sí, (No, no) hago la cama antes de salir.
3. Sí, (No, no) salgo con mis amigos después de clases.
4. Sí, (No, no) le doy un regalo a mi amigo para su cumpleaños.
5. Sí, (No, no) conozco tiendas donde venden ropa que está de moda.
6. Sí, (No, no) les digo siempre la verdad.
7. Sí, (No, no) me pongo el uniforme para jugar al béisbol.
8. Sí, (No, no) sé todos los secretos de mi mejor amigo(a).

⑤

1. Hago compras por Internet.
2. Tengo una falda nueva.
3. Me pongo la falda antes de ponerme la blusa.
4. Les doy regalos a mis amigos.
5. Traigo mis libros a clase.
6. Veo películas cómicas.

Did You Get It? Answer Key

PRÁCTICA DE GRAMÁTICA
PRONOUNS AFTER PREPOSITIONS, pp. 8–9

❶

1. ella
2. ti
3. él
4. ellas
5. nosotros
6. mí

❷

1. mí
2. ella
3. ellos(as)
4. nosotros(as)
5. ti/usted/ustedes/vosotros(as)

❸

1. A mí
2. A ti
3. A nosotros
4. A ellos/ellas
5. A él

❹

Answers will vary. Each must include one of the following verbs: **gustar**, **encantar**, **importar**, and **interesar**.

❺

1. Mi mamá va de compras conmigo.
2. Queremos comprar estas botas para ti.
3. A ti no te gusta esta falda.
4. ¿José, puedo ir contigo?
5. ¡La joyería está delante de nosotros!
6. ¡A mí me encanta la pulsera!

⬡ ¿RECUERDAS?
EXPRESSIONS OF FREQUENCY, p. 10

Práctica

❶

1. b
2. b
3. a
4. a
5. a

❷

Answers will vary. Possible answers limited to the following: **siempre**, **nunca**, **todos los días**, or **de vez en cuando**.

⬡ ¿RECUERDAS?
CLOTHING, p. 11

Práctica

1. Yo me pongo una camiseta en el verano.
2. Ellos se ponen los jeans cuando hace frío.
3. Nosotros nos ponemos un sombrero cuando hace sol.
4. Tú te pones una chaqueta cuando hace viento.
5. Ellos se ponen las botas cuando nieva.
6. Ustedes se ponen los pantalones cortos cuando hace mucho sol.

Did You Get It? Answer Key

PRÁCTICA DE VOCABULARIO
MARKET CRAFTS; COURTESY EXPRESSIONS, pp. 13–14

 ❶

1. una ganga
2. un retrato
3. una escultura única
4. un artículo hecho a mano
5. un artículo de oro
6. una pintura

❷

1. Con mucho gusto.
2. Es de metal.
3. Pase, por favor.
4. ¿Puedo entrar?
5. Sí, son muy finas.
6. De nada.

❸

1. de oro
2. fina
3. única
4. hecho a mano
5. de plata
6. baratos
7. ganga
8. de piedra
9. retrato
10. de madera

❹

1. Con permiso, ¿puedo ver esa pintura?
2. Con permiso, ¿puedo ver esa escultura de piedra?
3. Disculpe, ¿es de oro la pulsera?
4. De nada.
5. Perdóneme.
6. Estoy buscando artículos baratos.

❺

Answers will vary.

Did You Get It? Answer Key

PRÁCTICA DE GRAMÁTICA
IRREGULAR VERBS IN THE PRETERITE, pp. 16–17

1

1. estuve, estuvieron, estuviste, estuvimos, estuvo
2. tuvieron, tuvimos, tuvo, tuviste, tuve
3. puso, puse, pusimos, pusieron, puso
4. pudiste, pudo, pudieron, pudo, pudimos
5. tuvieron, tuve, tuvimos, tuvieron, tuvieron

2

1. estuvieron
2. pudieron
3. supimos
4. pusieron
5. tuvo
6. estuvieron
7. pusimos
8. tuvieron
9. supe
10. pudiste

3

1. estuvimos
2. supimos
3. pudimos
4. Tuvimos
5. puse
6. puso

4

1. Ella estuvo aquí ayer.
2. Supieron la verdad la semana pasada.
3. Lo (La) tuvimos el año pasado.
4. El señor Sánchez lo (la) puso allí ayer.
5. Por fin pudiste escribir el correo electrónico.
6. Lo supe ahora.
7. Estuvieron aquí la semana pasada.
8. Lo (La) tuvo el mes pasado.
9. Pudieron ir el martes.
10. Por fin se puso las botas.

Did You Get It? Answer Key

PRÁCTICA DE GRAMÁTICA

PRETERITE TENSE OF -*IR* STEM-CHANGING VERBS, pp. 19–20

1

1. pedí, pidieron, pidió
2. durmieron, dormimos, dormiste
3. seguiste, siguieron, siguió
4. preferiste, prefirió, prefirieron
5. servimos, sirvió, sirvieron
6. nos vestimos, se vistieron, te vestiste

2

1. pidió
2. compitió
3. dormimos
4. siguieron
5. sirvió
6. pidieron
7. Compitieron
8. nos vestimos
9. pidieron
10. prefirió

3

1. dormiste, duermes
2. compitieron, compiten
3. seguiste, sigues
4. pidió, pide
5. se vistió, se viste

4

1. Ellos pidieron pizza.
2. Yo me vestí temprano hoy.
3. Tú serviste una buena cena.
4. Emiliana durmió ocho horas.
5. Mis amigos compitieron en el campeonato.
6. Ella prefirió ir al cine.
7. Nosotros seguimos la lección.
8. El camarero sirvió una sopa fría.

¿RECUERDAS?

FAMILY MEMBERS AND CHORES, p. 21

Práctica

1. Mi mamá tuvo que barrer el suelo.
2. Mis hermanas tuvieron que lavar los platos.
3. Mi abuelo tuvo que cortar el césped.
4. Mi hermano y yo tuvimos que limpiar la cocina.
5. Yo tuve que sacar la basura.

¿RECUERDAS?

FOODS, p. 22

Práctica

1

1. d
2. f
3. g
4. c
5. i
6. j
7. a
8. h
9. e
10. b

2

Answers will vary but must include the verb pedir.

¡Más largo! *Práctica de vocabulario*

Find two words from the **Vocabulario** that contain the same letters and in the same order as the sequence and belong to the category stated.

Sequence	Category	Answers
1. MAC	stores	_____
2. DAR	verbs	_____
3. ADO	adjectives	_____
4. ERÍ	stores	_____

UNIDAD 3 Lección 1

Practice Games

Palabras escondidas *Vocabulario en contexto*

Use the following sentence to create words from the **Vocabulario**. There are at least thirteen possible answers. Can you find more?

Recomiendan las zapaterías.

1. _____
2. _____
3. _____
4. _____
5. _____

6. _____
7. _____
8. _____
9. _____
10. _____

11. _____
12. _____
13. _____
14. _____
15. _____

UNIDAD 3 Lección 1

Practice Games

¿Que le gusta a Diana? *Práctica de gramática 1*

Choose the correct irregular **yo** form of each verb. The boldfaced letters from the correct choices will spell out where Diana likes to go.

1. conocer

conoció   co**n**oce   **c**onozco

2. ver

ve**o**   **vo**y   vio

3. poner

pon**e**   pon   **p**ongo

4. traer

t**r**aigo   **tr**ajo   traje

5. hacer

hoy   h**a**go   hecho

6. salir

sal**e**   **s**algo   salió

Bonus: A Diana le gusta ir de ____ ____ m ____ ____ ____ ____

UNIDAD 3 Lección 1

Practice Games

¿Qué hacen? *Gramática en contexto*

Use the clues to fill in the missing letters of the irregular verbs to hear about Ángela's shopping trip.

1. Ángela y yo c ___ n ___ c ___ ___ ___ ___ todas las tiendas del centro.
2. Yo t ___ n ___ ___ que comprar mucha ropa para la fiesta.
3. Yo s ___ l ___ ___ de casa a las cinco.
4. Yo le d ___ ___ hoy el regalo a mamá.
5. Yo no s ___ cocinar bien el pescado.
6. Yo v ___ ___ la televisión después de la escuela todos los días.
7. Yo t ___ a ___ ___ ___ la música para la fiesta.

UNIDAD 3 Lección 1 Practice Games

Completa *Práctica de gramática 2*

Use the formula below to write complete sentences. Use the noun or pronoun after the preposition to add clarity or information. Hint: Remember that **a + el = al**, **de + el = del, con + ti = contigo**, and that **con + mi = conmigo**.

Modelo: el hotel : lejos de : el museo

El hotel está lejos del museo.

1. el zoológico : cerca de : el museo

_____

2. el pasaporte : para : Alejandro

_____

3. voy : de vacaciones : con : ti

_____

4. a ellos : gustar : las atracciones

_____

5. el hostal : al lado de : el mercado al aire libre

_____

6. Angelines : ir : con : mí : Perú

_____

7. Enrique : ir : a : el gimnasio : con : vosotros

_____

Tic-Tac-Toe *Todo junto*

Alone or with a friend, take turns finding the forms of the irregular **yo** forms in the boxes to see who wins at Tic-Tac-Toe. Place an **X** on the board over the correct answer for number 1. Then allow a partner to place an **O** over number 2. Play until someone has won.

X
1. Yo _____ las maletas.
3. Yo _____ a clase tarde.
5. Yo te _____ el regalo.
7. Yo _____ la verdad (*truth*) siempre.

O
2. Yo _____ la mesa.
4. Yo _____ cantar muy bien.
6. Yo _____ miedo de la montaña rusa.
8. Yo _____ a la maestra de arte.

digo	sabe	pongo
vengo	hago	sé
conozco	tengo	doy

Who won? _____

Copyright © by McDougal Littell, a division of Houghton Mifflin Company.

UNIDAD 3 Lección 1   Practice Games

¿Adónde va? *Lectura cultural*

Use the phrases to complete the sentences below and tell where Emilio goes.

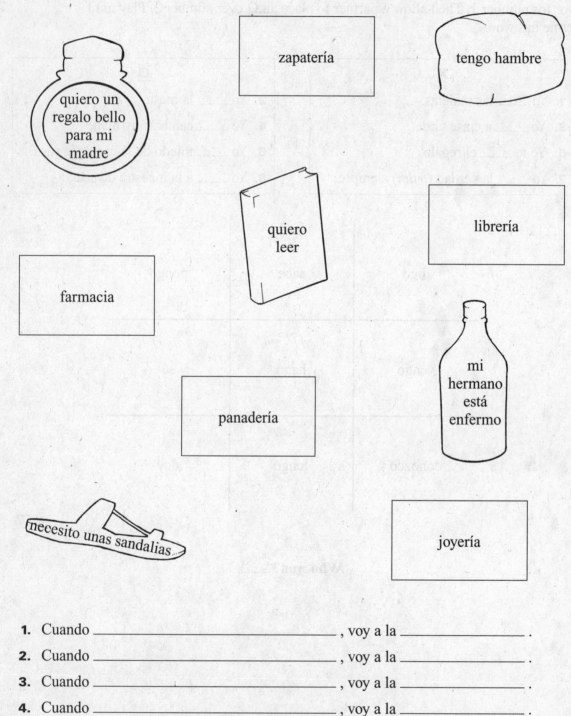

1. Cuando _____ , voy a la _____ .
2. Cuando _____ , voy a la _____ .
3. Cuando _____ , voy a la _____ .
4. Cuando _____ , voy a la _____ .
5. Cuando _____ , voy a la _____ .

Tienes... *Repaso de la lección*

Solve the sentence puzzles to figure out the seven-letter word that describes an old-fashioned clothing style. Hint: circle all the letters that the two words from **Vocabulario** have in common, then cross out those that are also in the third word.

Mi padre tiene un traje de ____ ____ ____ ____ ____ ____ ____.

1. This letter is in **almacén** and **chaleco**, but not in **pulsera**. ____
2. This letter is in **suéter** and **cinturón**, but not in **traje**. ____
3. This letter is in **abrigo** and **gorra**, but not in **reloj**. ____
4. This letter is in **falda** and **moda**, but not in **rayas**. ____
5. This letter is in **zapatería** and **número**, but not in **botas**. ____
6. This letter is in **demasiado** and **flojo**, but not in **mal**. ____
7. This letter is in **sandalias** and **pulsera**, but not in **talla**. ____

UNIDAD 3 Lección 1   Practice Games

Palabras escondidas *Práctica de vocabulario*

Use the following sentence to create words from the **Vocabulario**. There are at least fifteen possible answers. Can you find more? Hint: don't worry about accent marks.

¿Me deja tocar las pinturas?

1. _____   7. _____   13. _____
2. _____   8. _____   14. _____
3. _____   9. _____   15. _____
4. _____   10. _____   16. _____
5. _____   11. _____   17. _____
6. _____   12. _____

Sopa de palabras *Vocabulario en contexto*

Find the six materials hidden in the word search. Words run horizontally, vertically, and diagonally. Write them on the lines below.

```
L  B  C  A  L  N  J  É  Y  C  Y  M  A  Y
A  B  C  C  O  H  T  E  N  T  R  A  H  I
G  J  A  E  E  U  J  G  M  E  R  D  N  C
A  B  C  U  E  R  O  É  L  Z  P  E  Y  Y
M  A  N  P  E  C  Á  L  E  R  A  R  É  O
L  E  M  A  S  É  A  M  N  R  A  A  E  C
P  T  T  U  C  S  N  P  I  Y  Q  L  C  U
P  Y  V  A  I  B  G  P  L  C  U  L  H  R
L  U  G  D  L  E  C  I  I  E  A  J  A  S
A  D  A  N  E  H  P  I  E  D  R  A  S  P
T  O  L  T  C  H  E  F  L  F  L  D  O  A
A  V  Z  E  V  C  É  R  C  S  C  U  F  É
```

1. _____   4. _____

2. _____   5. _____

3. _____   6. _____

Now, write a sentence using as many as possible of the words you found.

_____

UNIDAD 3 Lección 2   Practice Games

El mercado al aire libre *Práctica de gramática 1*

What is Enrique looking for at the market? Choose the correct preterite form of each verb, and then put the bolded letters in order to find out.

1. poder: ellos

   pusieran   pudie**ro**n   pusiero**n**

2. estar: vosotros

   est**á**is   estuvie**ro**n   **e**stuvisteis

3. pagar: Tama y Jorge

   paga**b**an   pagaron   **p**egaron

4. mandar: Miguel y yo

   m**a**ndamos   mand**o**   mandas

5. lavar: él

   lav**é**   **l**avó   lav**o**

6. poner: Maribel

   pudo   pone   pus**o**

   Enrique busca un ____ ____ ____ ____ ____ ____ para su hermana.

Crucigrama *Gramática en contexto*

Use the correct irregular preterite conjugations to complete the sentences and fill in the crossword puzzle.

Horizontal (*Across*)

2. Enrique _____ la mesa hace cinco minutos.

4. Las chicas _____ del examen cinco minutos antes de clase.

5. Tú _____ los resultados del campeonato ayer, ¿verdad?

6. Yo _____ la comida en la cocina.

Abajo (*Down*)

1. Nosotros _____ que correr para coger el autobús.

2. Ana _____ ir a la fiesta conmigo.

3. Yo _____ en Barcelona para los Juegos Olímpicos de 1992.

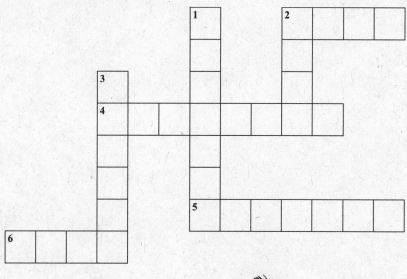

¿Qué piden y sirven? *Práctica de gramática 2*

Use the clues to fill in the missing letters of the preterite **-ir** stem-changing verbs to complete the sentences about Antonio's family dinner.

1. Anita y yo p ____ d ____ ____ ____ ____ pescado y patatas para la cena.

2. El camarero ____ i r ____ ____ ____ el postre al final.

3. Mamá se v ____ s ____ ____ ____ muy guapa.

4. Mis hermanos c ____ m p ____ t ____ ____ ____ r ____ ____ en comer rápido.

5. Yo no p ____ d ____ postre.

6. Todos nosotros s ____ g ____ ____ m ____ ____ a mi padre al coche.

7. Mis padres d ____ r ____ ____ e ____ ____ ____ muy bien.

Necesito... *Todo junto*

Solve the sentence puzzles to figure out the seven-letter word that states what you often have to ask for. Hint: circle all the letters that the two words from **Vocabulario** have in common, then eliminate those that are also in the third word.

____ ____ ____ ____ ____ ____ ____

1. This letter is in **plata** and **piedra**, but not in **metal**. ____
2. This letter is in **disculpe** and **hecho**, but not in **ganga**. ____
3. This letter is in **retrato** and **pintura**, but not in **plata**. ____
4. This letter is in **metal** and **cerámica**, but not in **barato**. ____
5. This letter is in **única** and **fina**, but not in **mano**. ____
6. This letter is in **pase** and **gusto**, but not in **nada**. ____
7. This letter is in **cuero** and **oro**, but not in **escultura**. ____

UNIDAD 3 Lección 2   Practice Games

Tic-Tac-Toe *Lectura cultural*

Alone or taking turns with a friend, find the correct preterite verbs in the boxes to see
which letter wins at Tic-Tac-Toe. Place an **X** on the board over the correct answer
for number 1. Then allow a partner to place an **O** over number 2. Play until X or O
appears three times in a row.

<table>
<tr><td colspan="2" align="center"><u>X</u></td></tr>
<tr><td>

1. Yo _____ pollo en la cena.

3. Ellos _____ en su cama en el hostal.

5. La mujer _____ muy guapa.

7. Nosotros _____ en la Copa Mundial.

</td></tr>
</table>

<table>
<tr><td align="center"><u>O</u></td></tr>
<tr><td>

2. Papá no _____ la verdad.

4. Nosotros _____ comer en el hotel.

6. El camarero _____ la comida.

8. ¿Tú _____ en la cafetería a la una?

</td></tr>
</table>

sirvió	competimos	pudimos
supo	se vistió	pedí
estuviste	pusiste	durmieron

Who won? _____

UNIDAD 3 Lección 2

Practice Games

44

Unidad 3, Lección 2
Practice Games

¡**Avancemos! 2**
Unit Resource Book

El alfabeto: A a Z *Repaso de la lección*

Use the letters of the alphabet to complete seven words and phrases from the **Vocabulario**. Use each letter only once.

A B C D E F G H I J L M N O P Q R S T U V Y

1. No ____ a ____ ____ e ____ ué.
2. M ____ d e ____ a ____ e r...
3. ____ a ____ g ____
4. e ____ ____ u ____ t ____ r a
5. C ____ n ____ e ____ ____ i s o.
6. ____ ____ n a
7. ____ a r a ____ o

Practice Games Answer Key

PAGE 30

Práctica de vocabulario

1. farmacia, almacén
2. quedarse, recomendar
3. cerrado, apretado
4. panadería, joyería, zapatería, librería

PAGE 31

Vocabulario en contexto

1. idea
2. mal/mala
3. apretado/apretada
4. moda
5. cerrado/cerrada
6. le encanta
7. importar
8. interesar
9. recomendar
10. parece
11. panadería
12. almacén
13. sandalias

PAGE 32

Práctica de gramática

1. conozco
2. veo
3. pongo
4. traigo
5. hago
6. salgo

Bonus: compras

PAGE 33

Gramática en contexto

1. conocemos
2. tengo
3. salgo
4. doy
5. sé
6. veo
7. traigo

Practice Games Answer Key

PAGE 34

Práctica de gramática 2

1. El zoológico está cerca del museo.
2. El pasaporte es para Alejandro.
3. Yo voy de vacaciones contigo.
4. A ellos les gustan las atracciones.
5. El hostal está al lado del mercado al aire libre.
6. Angelines va conmigo a Perú.
7. Enrique va al gimnasio con vosotros.

PAGE 35

Todo junto

X on hago, vengo, doy, digo

O on pongo, sé, tengo, conozco

Who won? X

PAGE 36

Lectura cultural

1. quiero un regalo bello para mi madre, joyería
2. necesito unas sandalias, zapatería
3. quiero leer, librería
4. mi hermano está enfermo, farmacia
5. tengo hambre, panadería

PAGE 37

Repaso de la lección

1. C
2. U
3. A
4. D
5. R
6. O
7. S

Practice Games Answer Key

PAGE 38

Práctica de vocabulario

1. perdón
2. nada
3. pase
4. disculpe
5. permiso
6. mano
7. cuero
8. madera
9. único/única
10. metal
11. plata
12. piedra
13. artículos
14. retrato

PAGE 39

Vocabulario en contexto

1. cerámica
2. cuero
3. madera
4. piedra
5. plata
6. metal

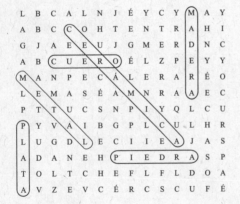

PAGE 40

Práctica de gramática 1

1. pudieron
2. estuvisteis
3. pagaron
4. mandamos
5. lavó
6. puso

Bonus: regalo

PAGE 41

Gramática en contexto

Horizontal	Vertical
2. puso	1. tuvimos
4. supieron	2. pudo
5. supiste	3. estuve
6. puse	

Practice Games Answer Key

PAGE 42

Práctica de gramática 2

1. pedimos
2. sirvió
3. vistió
4. compitieron
5. pedí
6. seguimos
7. durmieron

PAGE 43

Todo junto

1. P
2. E
3. R
4. M
5. I
6. S
7. O

PAGE 44

Lectura cultural

X on pedí, durmieron, se vistió, competimos

O on supo, pudimos, sirvió, estuviste

Who won? O

PAGE 45

Repaso de la lección

1. No hay de qué.
2. Me deja ver...
3. ganga
4. escultura
5. Con permiso.
6. fina
7. barato

Video Activities *Vocabulario*

PRE-VIEWING ACTIVITY

Answer the following questions about your clothing.

1 What are you wearing today?

_____

2 What factors principally influence what you decide to wear? The weather? Style? Comfort?

_____

3 Do you ever buy clothing that doesn't fit, just because you like it? Explain.

_____

4 Where do you go to buy your clothes?

_____

5 Do you like to shop?

_____

VIEWING ACTIVITY

Read the following activity before watching the video. Then, while you watch the video, use a check mark (✓) to indicate which items are first mentioned by Carolina or Emilio during their shopping trip.

Carolina	Emilio	
_____	_____	**1.** un reloj
_____	_____	**2.** un chaleco
_____	_____	**3.** un traje
_____	_____	**4.** una falda
_____	_____	**5.** una falda de cuadros
_____	_____	**6.** unas sandalias

UNIDAD 3 Lección 1

Video Activities

Video Activities *Vocabulario*

POST-VIEWING ACTIVITY

Put the following events in the correct order.

_____ Emilio se prueba un traje que le queda grande.

_____ Emilio recomienda una falda de cuadros.

_____ Emilio dice que la tienda está cerrada.

_____ Carolina se prueba una falda.

_____ Carolina quiere ir a una zapatería.

_____ Carolina se ríe del traje apretado de Emilio.

_____ Emilio necesita ir a una farmacia.

Video Activities *Telehistoria escena 1*

PRE-VIEWING ACTIVITY

Answer the following questions about what's in style.

1 Describe the clothing that was in style in another decade.

_____

2 Describe an outfit that was in style a few years ago.

_____

3 Describe an outfit that is in style right now.

_____

4 Is it most important to you to wear something that is in style, something that looks good on you, something that is comfortable or all of the above?

_____

VIEWING ACTIVITY

Read the sentences below before watching the video. Then, while you watch the video, indicate with a check mark (✓) whether each sentence refers to **Marta**, **Carolina** or **Álex**.

Marta	Carolina	Álex	
_____	_____	_____	**1.** El chaleco es para _____ .
_____	_____	_____	**2.** A _____ le encantan las rayas.
_____	_____	_____	**3.** Las sandalias son para _____ .
_____	_____	_____	**4.** Las botas son para _____ .
_____	_____	_____	**5.** _____ piensa ponerse una falda.
_____	_____	_____	**6.** A _____ le encanta el vestido rojo.

UNIDAD 3 Lección 1

Video Activities

Unidad 3, Lección 1
Video Activities

52

¡Avancemos! 2
Unit Resource Book

Video Activities *Telehistoria escena 1*

POST-VIEWING ACTIVITY

How would Carolina, Marta, and/or Álex answer each of the following questions? Choose the most appropriate answer to each question.

1. _____ ¿Qué piensas de este chaleco?

2. _____ Las rayas no están de moda. ¿Te gustan?

3. _____ ¿Vas a comprar los zapatos en la zapatería?

4. _____ Marta, ¿qué te pones de zapatos para la película?

5. _____ Álex, ¿Marta va a comprar tus zapatos?

6. _____ Carolina, ¿prefieres una falda?

7. _____ Carolina, ¿el vestido rojo está bien para la película?

8. _____ ¿Me queda bien el vestido?

a. Unas sandalias marrones, ¿no?

b. Sí. Esas botas están de moda.

c. Debe quedarle bien a Álex.

d. ¡No! Me parece una mala idea.

e. Sí, muy bien. A mí me encanta.

f. Sí. Voy al centro comercial más tarde.

g. Ya sé, pero ¡a mí me encantan!

h. Ay, no. Yo prefiero un vestido.

Video Activities *Telehistoria escena 2*

PRE-VIEWING ACTIVITY

You are shopping with your friend. What questions or statements could you say to your friend to help him or her make the right choice regarding an outfit to buy? Write five sentences commenting on the clothes he is wearing in the picture.

1 _____

_____

2 _____

_____

3 _____

_____

4 _____

_____

5 _____

_____

VIEWING ACTIVITY

Read the following statements before watching the video. Then, while watching the video, indicate with a check mark (✓) whether Marta, Carolina, or Alex makes or would make the statements.

Marta	Carolina	Álex	
_____	_____	_____	**1.** ¿Me lo pongo para la película?
_____	_____	_____	**2.** Aquí no se venden correas.
_____	_____	_____	**3.** En mi opinión te queda bien.
_____	_____	_____	**4.** ¿Te gusta Álex?
_____	_____	_____	**5.** Busco un chaleco más pequeño.
_____	_____	_____	**6.** ¿Te vas a vestir?
_____	_____	_____	**7.** No lo veo.

UNIDAD 3 Lección 1

Video Activities

Video Activities *Telehistoria escena 2*

POST-VIEWING ACTIVITY

Choose the word(s) that best complete(s) each of the following sentences, according to the video.

los pantalones	**el chaleco**	**el vestido de cuadros**
otra tienda	**un suéter nuevo**	**un vestido azul**
	un cinturón negro	

1. Marta busca _____ para comprar.

2. Carolina le trae _____ a Marta.

3. A Carolina no le gustan _____ que lleva Álex.

4. Álex necesita _____ .

5. Álex conoce _____ que tiene correas.

6. Carolina prefiere _____ .

7. Carolina piensa que _____ le queda grande a Álex.

UNIDAD 3 Lección 1

Video Activities

Video Activities *Telehistoria escena 3*

PRE-VIEWING ACTIVITY

Answer the following questions.

1 When you run errands, what type of transportation do you use?

_____

2 Where do you purchase any of these items?

toiletries: _____   shoes: _____

sporting clothes: _____   bread: _____

vitamins: _____   poultry/meat: _____

_____

3 What is your favorite store?

_____

4 What is one specialty store at which you shop? What do you buy there?

_____

VIEWING ACTIVITY

Read the list of events below before watching the video. Then, while you watch the video, put the events in the correct order.

_____ Álex le da dinero en efectivo a Carolina.

_____ Marta y Álex practican para la película.

_____ Marta y Álex van a almorzar.

_____ Carolina no puede pagar porque su dinero está en casa.

_____ Marta y Álex van a la zapatería.

_____ Todos se quedan en el mercado a las cuatro.

_____ Carolina recomienda la ropa que Álex y Marta se ponen para la película.

_____ Carolina le da la ropa para la película a Marta.

UNIDAD 3 Lección 1

Video Activities

Video Activities *Telehistoria escena 3*

POST-VIEWING ACTIVITY

Indicate if each of the following statements is true (T) or false (F).

1. Carolina va a darle el dinero después a Álex.   T   F

2. Carolina tiene otra ropa para la película que compró ayer.   T   F

3. Para la primera parte de la película Marta tiene un suéter y unos
pantalones.   T   F

4. La gorra que Carolina trae es para Álex.   T   F

5. Álex quiere ir de compras con Marta.   T   F

6. Marta le recomienda un buen restaurante a Álex que se llama la
Tortilla Azul.   T   F

7. Primero, Carolina tiene que ir a casa.   T   F

8. También Carolina tiene que ir a la farmacia y la panadería.   T   F

9. Álex le quiere ayudar a Carolina.   T   F

Video Activities *Vocabulario*

PRE-VIEWING ACTIVITY

1 Write four sentences describing and comparing the two pieces of art below. Then answer the following question.

Artesanía 1

Artesanía 2

_____

_____

_____

2 Which piece of art do you like best and why?

_____

VIEWING ACTIVITY

Before watching the video read the activity below. Then, watch the video.
Place a check mark (✓) on the phrase that best completes what happens in each circumstance.

1. Emilio casi rompe la escultura de…

_____ madera.

_____ metal.

_____ piedra.

2. El retrato es…

_____ muy caro.

_____ una ganga.

_____ barato.

3. Carolina mira una pulsera de…

_____ oro.

_____ plata.

_____ piedra.

UNIDAD 3 Lección 2 Video Activities

Copyright © by McDougal Littell, a division of Houghton Mifflin Company.

Unidad 3, Lección 2
Video Activities

58

¡Avancemos! 2
Unit Resource Book

Video Activities *Vocabulario*

POST-VIEWING ACTIVITY

Indicate if each of the following sentences is true (T) or false (F).
If the sentence is false, correct it on the line below.

1. Carolina y Emilio miran muchos artículos en el mercado. T   F
_____

2. Emilio y Carolina miran una escultura de oro.   T   F
_____

3. Carolina mira un retrato de un niño.   T   F
_____

4. Carolina mira una blusa fina.   T   F
_____

5. Emilio no compra la chaqueta de cuero porque es
una ganga.   T   F
_____

6. La joyería es única.   T   F
_____

7. La pulsera y el collar están hechos a mano.   T   F
_____

8. Carolina compra la pulsera de oro.   T   F
_____

Video Activities *Telehistoria escena 1*

PRE-VIEWING ACTIVITY

Answer the following questions.

1 How often do you arrive to places late?

_____

2 Have you ever forgotten about plans with someone?

_____

3 How would you react if a friend whom you had planned to meet did not come?

_____

VIEWING ACTIVITY

Read the following phrases before watching the video. Then, while watching the video, write **sí** (*yes*) if the statement is true and **no** (*no*) if the statement is false.

_____ **1.** Emilio no está y son las cuatro en punto.

_____ **2.** Empezamos cuando llega Emilio.

_____ **3.** La artesanía de la vendedora es de piedra.

_____ **4.** Carolina necesita la ayuda de Marta.

_____ **5.** Marta piensa que la pintura es bella pero muy cara.

_____ **6.** Marta no le está escuchando a Carolina.

_____ **7.** No pueden filmar porque Marta no tiene su suéter nuevo.

_____ **8.** Emilio acaba de hacer mucho ejercicio.

_____ **9.** Emilio perdió la cámara.

UNIDAD 3 Lección 2
Video Activities

60 Unidad 3, Lección 2
Video Activities

¡Avancemos! 2
Unit Resource Book

Video Activities *Telehistoria escena 1*

POST-VIEWING ACTIVITY

How would Carolina, Marta, and/or Álex answer each of the following questions?
Choose the most appropriate answer to each question.

1. _____ ¿Dónde está Emilio?

2. _____ ¿Qué hora es?

3. _____ Señora, ¿esto está hecho a mano?

4. _____ Es muy bello. ¿Cuánto cuesta?

5. _____ Álex, ¿qué piensas de esta pintura?

6. _____ Marta, ¿qué vamos a hacer ahora?

7. _____ ¿Por qué llegas tan tarde?

8. _____ Emilio, ¿qué pasó con la cámara?

a. Claro, lo hice yo.

b. No sé. Esta pintura a mí no me interesa.

c. No sé. Y él tiene la cámara.

d. Hace tres horas que camino por toda la ciudad.

e. Lo siento. La perdí.

f. Son las cuatro y media.

g. Es barato también. ¡Es una ganga!

h. Ay, perdón. ¿Qué me preguntaste?

UNIDAD 3 Lección 2

Video Activities

Video Activities *Telehistoria escena 2*

PRE-VIEWING ACTIVITY

When was the last time that you had a really busy day? Try to remember everything that you had to do that day. Describe the activities of your day in chronological order.

_____

_____

_____

_____

_____

_____

_____

VIEWING ACTIVITY

Read the list of places before watching the video. Then, while watching the video, indicate with a check mark (✓) which places **Emilio** has been to today.

Emilio estuvo en...

_____ la zapatería.

_____ la joyería.

_____ la farmacia.

_____ la panadería.

_____ unas tiendas.

_____ la librería.

_____ el almacén.

_____ el café.

_____ su casa.

UNIDAD 3 Lección 2

Video Activities

Unidad 3, Lección 2
Video Activities

62

¡Avancemos! 2
Unit Resource Book

Video Activities *Telehistoria escena 2*

POST-VIEWING ACTIVITY

Put the following events from Emilio's day in the correct order.

_____ Caminó por toda la ciudad buscando la cámara.

_____ La puso en su mochila y salió de casa.

_____ Llegó al mercado y habló con Marta y Carolina de la cámara.

_____ Compró un collar de oro para su madre.

_____ Emilio vio la cámara encima de la mesa.

_____ Almorzó en un café.

_____ Fue a la joyería.

Video Activities *Telehistoria escena 3*

PRE-VIEWING ACTIVITY

Answer the following questions about previous *Telehistoria* scenes with Marta, Carolina and Álex.

1 In previous scenes, do you notice anything unusual about Carolina's behavior?

_____

_____

2 Why do you think she is acting this way?

_____

_____

3 According to your answer to number 2, what do you think will happen in this episode?

_____

_____

4 What would you like to see happen in this episode?

_____

_____

VIEWING ACTIVITY

Read the sentences below before watching the video. Then, while you watch the video, indicate if each of the following statements is true (T) or false (F).

1.	Marta y Álex van al cine mañana.	T	F
2.	A Carolina no le gusta que Marta y Álex van al cine.	T	F
3.	En la película Marta está de compras en un mercado.	T	F
4.	Álex se llama Diego en la película.	T	F
5.	Marta y Álex se vistieron para la segunda parte de la película.	T	F
6.	Carolina le dio un suéter y una falda a Marta para la primera parte.	T	F
7.	Álex le pregunta a Carolina si quiere ir al cine con él.	T	F
8.	A Carolina le encantaría ir al cine con Álex.	T	F

UNIDAD 3 Lección 2

Video Activities

Video Activities *Telehistoria escena 3*

POST-VIEWING ACTIVITY

Complete each sentence by choosing the person who does each activity.

1. _____ habla con Jeny por teléfono celular.

   a. Marta

   b. Álex

   c. Carolina

2. _____ habla con su madre por teléfono celular.

   a. Marta

   b. Álex

   c. Carolina

3. _____ le pregunta a Jeny si quiere ir al cine.

   a. Marta

   b. Álex

   c. Carolina

4. _____ piensa que Marta y Álex van al cine mañana.

   a. Marta

   b. Álex

   c. Carolina

5. Carolina le dio un suéter nuevo a _____ para la primera parte.

   a. Marta

   b. Álex

   c. Jeny

6. Álex le pregunta a _____ si ella quiere ir al cine mañana.

   a. Marta

   b. Álex

   c. Carolina

UNIDAD 3 Lección 2   Video Activities

Video Activities Answer Key

VOCABULARIO pp. 50–51

PRE-VIEWING ACTIVITY

Answers will vary. Possible answers:

1. I'm wearing jeans, a T-shirt, socks and tennis shoes.
2. The weather.
3. No. I only buy comfortable clothing.
4. I buy my clothes at department stores.
5. I like to shop with my friends.

VIEWING ACTIVITY

1. Emilio
2. Carolina
3. Emilio
4. Carolina
5. Emilio
6. Carolina

POST-VIEWING ACTIVITY

Emilio se prueba un traje que le queda grande. __2__

Emilio recomienda una falda de cuadros. __5__

La tienda está cerrada. __1__

Carolina se prueba una falda. __4__

Carolina quiere ir a una zapatería. __6__

Carolina se ríe del traje apretado de Emilio. __3__

Emilio necesita ir a una farmacia. __7__

TELEHISTORIA ESCENA 1 pp. 52–53

PRE-VIEWING ACTIVITY

Answers will vary. Possible answers:

1. In the 1960s, it was in style to wear very informal clothes with a lot of flowers.
2. A fitted T-shirt, baggy jeans and popular sneakers.
3. A concert T-shirt with a western belt and rolled up, fitted jeans. For shoes: leather flats.
4. Ideally, I would like to buy something that is all of the above!

VIEWING ACTIVITY

1. Álex
2. Carolina
3. Marta
4. Álex
5. Marta
6. Álex

POST-VIEWING ACTIVITY

1. c
2. g
3. f
4. a
5. b
6. h
7. d
8. e

TELEHISTORIA ESCENA 2 pp. 54–55

PRE-VIEWING ACTIVITY

Answers will vary. Possible answers:

1. Carlos! Your outfit doesn't match.
2. Why don't you try on some smaller pants? Those are too big for you.
3. You should try on a striped jacket. It will go better with the pants.
4. I think you should try on the sneakers with that outfit.
5. If you put the belt on, the pants might fit you better.

VIEWING ACTIVITY

1. Marta
2. Álex
3. Álex
4. Carolina
5. Álex
6. Carolina
7. Carolina

POST-VIEWING ACTIVITY

1. un suéter nuevo
2. un vestido azul
3. los pantalones
4. un cinturón negro
5. otra tienda
6. el vestido de cuadros
7. el chaleco

TELEHISTORIA ESCENA 3 pp. 56–57

PRE-VIEWING ACTIVITY

Answers will vary. Possible answers:

1. I usually ride my bike when I run errands.
2. toiletries: the grocery store; shoes: the shoe store in the mall; sporting clothes: a sporting goods store; bread: the grocery store; vitamins: the grocery store; poultry/meat: the meat market
3. My favorite store is _____.
4. I shop at an art store to buy paint brushes, acrylic paint and canvases.

VIEWING ACTIVITY

Álex le da dinero en efectivo a Carolina. __3__

Marta y Álex practican para la película. __7__

Marta y Álex van a almorzar. __6__

Carolina no puede pagar porque su dinero está en casa. __2__

Marta y Álex van a la zapatería. __5__

Todos se quedan en el mercado a las cuatro. __8__

Carolina recomienda la ropa que Álex y Marta se ponen para la película. __1__

Carolina le da la ropa para la película a Marta. __4__

POST-VIEWING ACTIVITY

1. T
2. F
3. T
4. T
5. T
6. F
7. T
8. F
9. T

Copyright © by McDougal Littell, a division of Houghton Mifflin Company.

Video Activities Answer Key

VOCABULARIO pp. 58–59

PRE-VIEWING ACTIVITY

Answers will vary.

VIEWING ACTIVITY

1. piedra ☐
2. muy caro ☐
3. oro ☐

POST-VIEWING ACTIVITY

1. T
2. F; Miran esculturas de piedra, madera y metal, no de oro.
3. F; Mira un retrato de una mujer bonita.
4. T
5. F; No compra la chaqueta porque es demasiado cara.
6. T
7. T
8. F; Carolina le da la pulsera al hombre.

TELEHISTORIA ESCENA 1 pp. 60–61

PRE-VIEWING ACTIVITY

Answers will vary. Possible answers:

1. I rarely arrive places late.
2. No, I have never forgotten about plans with someone else.
3. I would be very upset.

VIEWING ACTIVITY

1. no
2. sí
3. no
4. sí
5. sí
6. sí
7. no
8. no
9. sí

POST-VIEWING ACTIVITY

1. c
2. f
3. a
4. g
5. b
6. h
7. d
8. e

TELEHISTORIA ESCENA 2 pp. 62–63

PRE-VIEWING ACTIVITY

Answers will vary.

VIEWING ACTIVITY

la joyería. ☐
la panadería. ☐
unas tiendas. ☐
el café. ☐
su casa. ☐

POST-VIEWING ACTIVITY

Caminó por toda la ciudad buscando la cámara. **6**

La puso en su mochila y salió de casa. **2**

Llegó al mercado y habló con Marta y Carolina de la cámara. **7**

Compró un collar de oro para su madre. **4**

Emilio vio la cámara encima de la mesa. **1**

Almorzó en un café. **5**

Fue a la joyería. **3**

TELEHISTORIA ESCENA 3 pp. 64–65

PRE-VIEWING ACTIVITY

Answers will vary. Possible answers:

1. Yes, she seems to be more upset than she should be in many situations.
2. I think that she is jealous of Marta because Álex likes Marta.
3. I think that Marta and Álex will go looking for the camera with Emilio. When they hang out together, they will decide that they like each other and start dating.
4. I would like to see Carolina and Álex get together because Carolina likes Álex so much.

VIEWING ACTIVITY

1. F
2. T
3. T
4. F
5. T
6. F
7. T
8. T

POST-VIEWING ACTIVITY

1. a
2. b
3. a
4. c
5. a
6. c

Copyright © by McDougal Littell, a division of Houghton Mifflin Company.

UNIDAD 3 Lección 2   Video Activities Answer Key

Video Scripts

VOCABULARIO

Carolina: ¡Hola! Soy Carolina.

Emilio: Y yo me llamo Emilio.

Carolina: Hoy vamos… ¡de compras!

Emilio: ¡Está cerrado!

Carolina: No, está abierto.

Emilio: Aquí puedes comprar un reloj.

Carolina: O una gorra.

Emilio: También puedes comprar un cinturón. O como decimos aquí en Puerto Rico, una correa.

Carolina: O un chaleco.

Emilio: ¿Cómo me queda este traje?

Carolina: Te queda mal. Es demasiado grande.

Emilio: ¿Me queda grande?

Carolina: Creo que sí.

Emilio: Y éste, me queda demasiado apretado, ¿no?

Carolina: No, te queda muy bien.

Carolina: ¿Te gusta esta falda? Yo prefiero la falda de rayas.

Emilio: Pues, yo te recomiendo ésta.

Carolina: ¿De cuadros? ¡Ay, no! ¡No me gusta la ropa de cuadros! Estas sandalias me gustan pero no me quedan bien. No son mi número. ¿Podemos ir a una zapatería?

Emilio: Sí.

Carolina: ¿Y después a la joyería?

Emilio: ¿Qué?

Carolina: ¿Y después a la librería?

Emilio: Creo que no.

Carolina: ¿Por qué no?

Emilio: Necesito ir a la farmacia.

Carolina: ¿A la farmacia? ¿Por qué?

Emilio: Tengo que comprar aspirina.

Carolina: ¿Aspirina? ¿Por qué?

Emilio: Porque después de pasar el día en la tienda de ropa, en la zapatería, y en la joyería, ¡me va a doler la cabeza!

TELEHISTORIA ESCENA 1

Carolina: Este chaleco debe quedarle bien a Álex.

Marta: Sí, pero, ¿te gustan las rayas?… No están de moda.

Carolina: Yo sé, pero ¡a mí me encantan las rayas!

Marta: Pues, tú sabes mejor que yo. Tú eres la directora.

Carolina: Tenemos el chaleco de Álex. Ahora necesitamos tus sandalias y las botas de Álex.

Marta: Puedo comprarlas más tarde en la zapatería, en el centro comercial.

Carolina: ¿Ah, sí? ¡Gracias!

Marta: Y yo… ¿Me pongo una falda para la película? ¿O prefieres los vestidos?

Carolina: Hmmm… creo que sí, prefiero los vestidos.

Marta: ¿Cómo me queda este vestido? ¿Está bien para la película?

Carolina: En mi opinión… es una mala idea. ¡Es muy… *rojo*!

Marta: ¿Muy *rojo*? Pero me parece que a Álex le encanta.

Video Scripts

TELEHISTORIA ESCENA 2

Carolina: ¿Te gusta Álex? ¿Sí?

Marta: ¿Qué? ¿Dónde está el nuevo suéter que quiero comprar?

Carolina: No sé... no lo veo. Mira, aquí te traigo un vestido azul. Ay no, Álex, ¡no me gustan esos pantalones! ¡Y el chaleco te queda demasiado grande!

Álex: Entonces, voy a buscar otros pantalones y un chaleco más pequeño.

Carolina: Está bien. También necesitas una correa negra.

Álex: Aquí no hay. Pero conozco una tienda donde podemos comprar una.

Carolina: ¡Perfecto! Marta, ¿te vas a vestir? Quiero ver cómo te queda el vestido.

Marta: ¡Ahora salgo! ¿Me pongo esto para la película?

Álex: Te queda bien.

Carolina: ¡No! Prefiero este vestido de cuadros.

TELEHISTORIA ESCENA 3

Álex: ¿Qué pasa, Carolina?

Carolina: ¡Ay! No encuentro mi dinero. Debe estar en casa.

Álex: Yo traigo dinero. ¿Lo necesitas?

Carolina: Gracias, Álex. ¡Pero te doy el dinero después! ¿Qué hora es? No tengo mi reloj.

Marta: Son las once.

Álex: Son las once. Filmamos a las cuatro en el mercado, ¿no?

Carolina: Sí. Tengo otra ropa aquí de mi casa. El suéter y los pantalones son para ti, para la primera parte de la película, y la gorra es para él.

Marta: ¿Quieren ir de compras conmigo? Voy a la zapatería.

Álex: Bueno, sí, y podemos almorzar después.

Marta: Sí, te voy a recomendar un restaurante muy bueno. Conozco uno que se llama Las Flores.

Álex: Sí, sé dónde está. ¿Vienes con nosotros?

Carolina: No, tengo que ir a casa y después a la joyería, luego a la farmacia...

Álex: Entiendo. ¿Te ayudamos? Podemos ir contigo...

Carolina: Creo que no, Álex, pero gracias. Mi casa queda lejos de aquí y ustedes deben almorzar.

Marta: Sí, y Álex y yo debemos practicar para la película! «¿Viene conmigo a la zapatería, señor Álex?»

Álex: «Está bien.» Nos vemos a las cuatro.

Carolina: Está bien.

Video Scripts

VOCABULARIO

Carolina: Aquí venden artesanías.

Emilio: Podemos comprar muchos artículos aquí.

Carolina: Este señor hace esculturas. Señor, ¿me deja ver esa escultura?

Vendedor: Con mucho gusto, señorita.

Carolina: Esta escultura es de metal.

Emilio: Y esta otra es de madera.

Carolina: Mira ésta: es de piedra. ¡Emilio!

Emilio: Lo siento mucho.

Carolina: Aquí podemos comprar pinturas.

Emilio: ¡Qué bello es este retrato! Es el retrato de una mujer bonita.

Emilio: ¡Mira! ¡Es una ganga!

Emilio: ¡Qué caro!

Carolina: Disculpe, señor.

Carolina: Vamos a ver la ropa. Esta blusa es muy fina.

Emilio: Esta chaqueta es de cuero. Me gusta mucho, y me queda bien, pero es demasiado caro.

Carolina: ¡Emilio!

Emilio: ¡Perdóneme!

Carolina: Esta joyería es única. Disculpe, ¿me deja ver esta pulsera y aquel collar?

Vendedora: Claro que sí.

Carolina: ¿Están hechos a mano?

Vendedora: Sí. Los hice yo. La pulsera es de oro y el collar es de plata.

Emilio: Son muy bellos. Gracias.

Vendedora: De nada.

Carolina: ¡Adiós!

Emilio: ¡Hasta luego!

Vendedor 2: Perdón muchacho. Perdón.

Emilio: Carolina, ¿me ayudas, por favor? Gracias.

Carolina: No hay de qué.

TELEHISTORIA ESCENA 1

Carolina: ¿Dónde está Emilio? ¡Son las cuatro y media! No podemos empezar porque él tiene la cámara.

Marta: Perdón, señoria, ¿esto está hecho a mano?

Vendedor: Sí, señorita. Es de plata. Y es muy barato.

Marta: ¡Qué bello!

Carolina: Marta, ¿me puedes ayudar por favor? ¡Puedes ver las artesanías después!

Marta: Esta pintura es muy bella también. ¿Te gusta? ¡Ay, pero qué cara!

Carolina: ¡Marta! ¡Escucha! ¡No tenemos cámara! ¿Qué vamos a hacer ahora?

Marta: Ay, perdón. ¿Qué me preguntaste? Mira, allí viene Emilio.

Emilio: Lo siento. Hace tres horas que camino por toda la ciudad.

Carolina: ¿Y por qué? ¿Para hacer ejercicio?

Emilio: No, para buscar la cámara. La perdí.

TELEHISTORIA ESCENA 2

Emilio: La vi encima de la mesa en casa hoy por la mañana. La puse en mi mochila y salí.

Marta: ¿Y no sabes cuándo la perdiste?

Emilio: No sé cuándo la perdí. Lo siento mucho. Primero fui a comprar un regalo de cumpleaños para mi madre: este collar. ¡Es de oro y fue una ganga! Hace un año que le compré una pulsera...

Video Scripts

Carolina: ¡Emilio! ¡La cámara!

Emilio: ¡Perdón! Estuve un rato en la joyería, después fui a unas tiendas, y más tarde comí en un café.

Marta: ¿Y llevaste la cámara contigo?

Emilio: ¡No sé! Volvíal café y a las tiendas, pero no pude encontrarla.

Carolina: ¿Qué estás comiendo?

Emilio: Una galleta… de la panadería… ¡La panadería!

TELEHISTORIA ESCENA 3

Marta: ¿Quieres ir al cine mañana?

Álex: Buena idea.

Carolina: Vamos a comenzar…

Marta: Nos vemos mañana, Jeny.

Álex: Hasta luego, mamá.

Carolina: ¿Okay? ¡Acción!

Marta: Con permiso. ¿Me deja ver esa escultura de piedra?

Álex: Con mucho gusto, señorita.

Marta: Es muy fina. ¿Está hecha a mano?

Álex: Sí, yo la hice.

Marta: Entonces, ¿es única?

Álex: Sí, es única, como usted. Yo me llamo Daniel.

Marta: Y yo soy Ariana.

Carolina: ¡Un momento! Marta, Álex, ¿por qué se pusieron esa ropa? ¡Ustedes se vistieron para la segunda parte de la película!

Marta: ¡Ay! ¡Tienes razón! Me diste un suéter y unos pantalones para la primera parte. Este vestido es para después. ¡Lo siento!

Álex: Carolina, ¿quieres ir al cine conmigo mañana?

Carolina: Pero... pero, ¿no vas con Marta? ¿Ella no te preguntó... ?

Álex: ¿Marta? ¡No! Ella no me preguntó nada. Ella va con Jeny. Me gustaría ir contigo.

Carolina: Entonces, ¡sí!

Álex: ¡Perfecto! Hablamos mañana.

COMPARACIÓN CULTURAL VIDEO

Shopping is fun everywhere, but shopping for arts and crafts in the Spanish-speaking world is also a great way to learn about the country's traditions. Here you will see different types of arts and crafts sold in markets, like masks in Puerto Rico, scarves and fabrics in Ecuador, and jewelry from Costa Rica.

Puerto Rico

In a traditional arts and craft market in Puerto Rico you can find jewelry made from wood, beads and wire…hand-painted boxes…rag dolls…and typical percussion instruments.

You can also find these masks. They are made from papier-mâché or coconut shells. People wear them at carnavals or hang them on the wall as decorations.

Ecuador

El Ejido Market, in Quito, Ecuador, is a good place to shop for wool sweaters, hats, scarves and other colorful clothing items. In Ecuador, selling arts and crafts is often a family business. In some markets you can also find typical snacks for sale.

Costa Rica

In Costa Rican markets, handmade jewelry is very popular. They offer a huge variety of unique items. Prices vary from artisan to artisan, but you can usually find a good deal.

Every country has a distinctive style of arts and crafts defined by the available materials in the country and the artisans' skills. You saw traditional masks in Puerto Rico, colorful fabrics in Ecuador, and jewelry from Costa Rica. What would you advise someone to buy if they visited your city?

Audio Scripts

Copyright © by McDougal Littell, a division of Houghton Mifflin Company.

UNIDAD 3, LECCIÓN 1
TEXTBOOK SCRIPTS
TXT CD 4

PRESENTACIÓN DE VOCABULARIO

Level 2 Textbook pp. 144–145

TXT CD 4, Track 1

A. ¡Hola! Soy Emilio. ¿Es buena idea ir de compras con una amiga? A mi amiga Carolina siempre le gusta vestirse con la ropa más nueva, ropa que está de moda. Pero en mi opinión, es mala idea vestirte con ropa que está de moda si la ropa no te queda bien.

B. Encontrar la talla correcta no es siempre fácil. ¿Cómo me quedan estos tres trajes? ¿Cuál me recomiendas? El traje verde es demasiado grande; me queda flojo. El traje marrón es muy pequeño; me queda apretado. ¡El traje gris me queda muy bien! ¿Lo compro? ¡Creo que sí!

C. Carolina va a la joyería para ver las joyas y tal vez comprar una pulsera. Yo voy a la librería para comprar un libro. Luego, vamos los dos a la zapatería. Ella quiere comprar unos zapatos y yo unas botas.

D. También tenemos que comprar champú, pero la farmacia está cerrada. Entonces vamos a la panadería y vemos que está abierta. ¡Qué bien! Entramos para comprar pan para la cena.

E. Si las tiendas están cerradas, a Carolina le encanta hacer las compras por Internet porque, ¡siempre está abierto!

¡A RESPONDER!

Level 2 Textbook p. 145

TXT CD 4, Track 2

Escucha y decide si llevas la ropa o el objeto en las siguientes descripciones. Indica la ropa o el objeto si lo llevas.

1. Llevo un cinturón.
2. Llevo una falda.
3. Llevo un reloj hoy.
4. Llevo una pulsera.
5. Llevo sandalias.
6. Llevo botas.
7. Llevo ropa de cuadros.
8. Llevo ropa de rayas.

TELEHISTORIA ESCENA 1

Level 2 Textbook p. 147

TXT CD 4, Track 3

Carolina: Este chaleco debe quedarle bien a Álex.

Marta: Sí, pero, ¿te gustan las rayas? No están de moda.

Carolina: Yo sé, pero, ¡a mí me encantan las rayas!

Marta: Pues tú sabes mejor que yo. Tú eres la directora.

Carolina: Tenemos el chaleco de Álex. Ahora necesitamos tus sandalias y las botas de Álex.

Marta: Puedo comprarlas más tarde en la zapatería, en el centro comercial.

Carolina: ¿Ah, sí? ¡Gracias!

Marta: Y yo... ¿Me pongo una falda para la película? ¿O prefieres los vestidos?

Carolina: Hmm... creo que sí, prefiero los vestidos.

Marta: ¿Cómo me queda este vestido? ¿Está bien para la película?

Carolina: En mi opinión... es una mala idea. ¡Es muy... rojo!

Marta: ¿Muy rojo? Pero me parece que a Álex le encanta.

ACTIVIDAD 7 - LAS FIESTAS

Level 2 Textbook p. 150

TXT CD 4, Track 4

Indica qué hace Carolina para la fiesta.

A veces doy fiestas pequeñas en mi casa para mis amigos. Antes de la fiesta, mi hermana limpia la sala y yo pongo la mesa. También hago todas las decoraciones. Después, salgo a la tienda para comprar los refrescos. Normalmente mi mamá hace un pastel, pero si no tiene tiempo, yo traigo galletas de la tienda.

A la hora de la fiesta, vienen todos mis amigos de la escuela, y a veces vienen también mis primos. ¡Es tan divertido! No veo mucho a mis primos porque viven lejos, pero siempre vienen para las fiestas y salen muy tarde de la casa.

TELEHISTORIA ESCENA 2

Level 2 Textbook p. 152

TXT CD 4, Track 5

Carolina: ¿Te gusta Álex? ¿Sí?

Marta: ¿Qué? ¿Dónde está el nuevo suéter que quiero comprar?

Carolina: No sé... no lo veo. Mira, aquí te traigo un vestido azul. Ay no, Álex, ¡no me gustan esos pantalones! ¡Y el chaleco te queda demasiado grande!

Álex: Entonces voy a buscar otros pantalones y un chaleco más pequeño.

Carolina: Está bien. También necesitas una correa negra.

Álex: Aquí no hay. Pero conozco una tienda donde podemos comprar una.

Carolina: ¡Perfecto! Marta, ¿te vas a vestir? Quiero ver cómo te queda el vestido.

Marta: ¡Ahora salgo! ¿Me pongo esto para la película?

Álex: Te queda bien.

Carolina: ¡No...! Prefiero este vestido de cuadros.

PRONUNCIACIÓN

Level 2 Textbook p. 155

TXT CD 4, Track 6

Diptongos

In Spanish, the strong vowels are **a, e,** and **o**; the weak vowels are **i** and **u**. A diphthong is the combination of a weak and a strong vowel or two weak vowels. These combinations create one sound and therefore one syllable. Listen and repeat, noting the sounds of the diphthongs in these words.

Audio Scripts

afeitar
aduana
interior
abierto
luego
farmacia

TELEHISTORIA COMPLETA

Level 2 Textbook p. 157

TXT CD 4, Track 7

Escena 1 Resumen

Narrator: Carolina y Marta buscan ropa para su película. Álex está con ellas. A Carolina le gusta Álex, pero ella piensa que a Álex le gusta Marta.

Escena 2 Resumen

Marta y Álex se ponen la ropa para la película. Carolina les da su opinión sobre la ropa.

Escena 3

Carolina: ¡Ay! No encuentro mi dinero. Debe estar en casa.

Álex: Yo traigo dinero. ¿Lo necesitas?

Carolina: Gracias, Álex. ¡Pero te doy el dinero después! ¿Qué hora es? No tengo mi reloj.

Marta: Son las once.

Álex: Filmamos a las cuatro en el mercado, ¿no?

Carolina: Sí. Tengo otra ropa aquí de mi casa. El suéter y los pantalones son para ti, para la primera parte de la película, y la gorra es para él.

Marta: ¿Quieren ir de compras conmigo? Voy a la zapatería.

Álex: Bueno, sí, y podemos almorzar después.

Marta: Sí, te voy a recomendar un restaurante muy bueno. Conozco uno que se llama Las Flores.

Álex: Sí, sé dónde está. ¿Vienes con nosotros?

Carolina: No, tengo que ir a casa y después a la joyería, luego a la farmacia...

Álex: Entiendo. ¿Te ayudamos?

Carolina: Creo que no, Álex, pero gracias. Mi casa queda lejos de aquí y ustedes deben almorzar.

Marta: Sí, y Álex y yo debemos practicar para la película. «¿Viene conmigo a la zapatería, señor Álex?»

Álex: «Está bien». Nos vemos a las cuatro.

Carolina: Está bien.

ACTIVIDAD 20 – INTEGRACIÓN

Level 2 Textbook p. 159

TXT CD 4, Track 8

Lee el anuncio y llama a una zapatería para saber su horario y dónde queda. Después recomiéndale un plan a tu amigo(a) para ir de compras con él o ella. Incluye el día, los lugares, las horas, lo que piensas comprar y para quiénes.

FUENTE 2

TXT CD 4, Track 9

Listen and take notes.

¿Dónde queda Zapatolandia?

¿Cuándo está abierto? ¿Cuándo está cerrado?

¿Por qué debes llevar un amigo contigo si vas este domingo?

Bienvenidos a Zapatolandia, la zapatería que vende todo lo nuevo en zapatos, botas y sandalias para hombres y mujeres, y siempre a precios bajos. Nos puedes encontrar en el centro comercial Plaza Las Palmas entre la librería Fuentes y la farmacia Minimax. Estamos abiertos de lunes a sábado de las nueve de la mañana a las nueve de la noche, y los domingos de las doce a las cinco de la tarde. Este domingo 22 de noviembre recibes dos pares de zapatos por el precio de uno. ¡Trae a un amigo contigo! ¡Les van a encantar nuestros zapatos y nuestras gangas!

LECTURA: REVISTA DE MODA

Level 2 Textbook pp. 160–161

TXT CD 4, Track 10

¿Estás cansado de buscar tu ropa en un clóset desorganizado? Este artículo presenta ideas que te van a ayudar.

¡Organiza tu clóset!

Tener un clóset organizado te lo hace todo más fácil.

Primero, saca todo lo que tienes del clóset. Separa la ropa que usas mucho de la ropa que casi no usas.

De la ropa que no usas frecuentemente, escoge lo que ya no está de moda o lo que ya no te queda. Pon toda esta ropa en una bolsa de plástico y dásela a una organización filantrópica.

1. La ropa formal, como vestidos o trajes: Debes guardarla en plástico a un lado del clóset. Debes colgar al otro lado la ropa que más usas.

2. Camisas, blusas, chalecos: Organízalos por colores y tipo de ropa.

3. Jeans y pantalones: Puedes doblar y colgarlos en ganchos de varios niveles para tener más espacio. Muchachas, es buena idea hacer esto con las faldas también. Si tienes estantes en el clóset, debes poner allí la ropa que puedes doblar.

   Para los que viven lejos de su país tropical, también deben tener ropa para el frío. Durante el invierno, guarda toda tu ropa de verano en una maleta o caja. Durante el verano, guarda la ropa de invierno en la maleta donde guardaste la ropa de verano.

4. Camisetas: Organízalas por colores y tipos.

5. Ropa deportiva: Pon toda tu ropa de ejercicio en un lugar.

6. Suéteres: Ponlos todos juntos y organízalos por colores y tipos.

7. Abrigos: Puedes colgar los que usas frecuentemente en un gancho en la puerta. Puedes colgar los otros al fondo del clóset.

8. Zapatos: Guarda tus zapatos más caros y botas altas en sus cajas en el piso. Para los otros, usa un estante.

9. Usa un gancho largo en la puerta para colgar tus correas y otras cosas.

10. En la parte de arriba, puedes guardar: (muchachos) tu mochila, tus gorras y cosas extras; (muchachas) tu mochila, tus carteras y otros accesorios.

Audio Scripts

REPASO: ACTIVIDAD 1 - LISTEN AND UNDERSTAND

Level 2 Textbook p. 164

TXT CD 4, Track 11

Escucha a estas personas y decide dónde van de compras.

1. Me gustan las botas negras. Necesito un número nueve.
2. No me interesan las pulseras, pero quiero comprar un anillo.
3. No encuentro mi talla en esta falda de rayas. Pues no me importa. Voy a buscar otra.
4. Tengo hambre. Me encanta el pan que venden aquí. ¡Qué rico!
5. Me interesan los libros de ciencias. ¿Hay unos aquí?
6. Necesito comprar desodorante y un cepillo de dientes nuevo.

WORKBOOK SCRIPTS
WB CD 2

INTEGRACIÓN HABLAR

Level 2 Workbook p. 108

WB CD 2, Track 1

Escucha el anuncio que sale por altoparlante. Toma apuntes.

FUENTE 2

WB CD 2, Track 2

¡Bienvenidos! Veo que a todos ustedes les encanta vestirse con ropa que está de moda. A las chicas les encantan los zapatos y las botas. Para ellas tenemos una nuevas botas muy bellas. A los chicos también les importa la moda. Para ellos tenemos abrigos de cuadros y chalecos de rayas. ¡Toda la ropa de nuestra nueva colección está muy de moda!

INTEGRACIÓN ESCRIBIR

Level 2 Workbook p. 109

WB CD 2, Track 3

Escucha a la señora Mirta hablando de la tienda en su programa de televisión. Toma apuntes.

FUENTE 2

WB CD 2, Track 4

¡Buenos días! Tengo un programa especial para ustedes. Vamos a hablar de la moda. Voy a invitar a seis de ustedes —chicos y chicas— para vestirse con ropa, joyas y zapatos nuevos para ver si les quedan mejor que lo que llevan. Todo viene de mis tiendas favoritas: Siempre me pongo cosas de allí. Hoy llevo botas altas de «Pies Perfectos», aretes y una pulsera de «Tesoros para ti» y una falda de rayas con un suéter flojo de «Ropa Loca». ¿Me quedan bien? Ahora, ¡empezamos!

ESCUCHAR A, ACTIVIDAD 1

Level 2 Workbook p. 110

WB CD 2, Track 5

Escucha a Pedro. Después, lee las oraciones y contesta cierto o falso.

Pedro: Hola, soy Pedro. El viernes voy a dar una fiesta y tengo que comprarme un traje nuevo. Necesito un traje de la talla correcta porque no me gusta cuando los trajes me quedan flojos, y no me gustan cuando me quedan apretados. A veces, me parece que es muy difícil encontrar el traje ideal para mí. Tengo un traje negro que me encanta, pero ya es muy viejo. Ahora voy de compras con mi hermano mayor. Él se viste siempre con ropa de moda y viene conmigo para recomendarme algo.

ESCUCHAR A, ACTIVIDAD 2

Level 2 Workbook p. 110

WB CD 2, Track 6

Escucha a Luis. Luego, contesta las preguntas.

Luis: Buenos días. Me llamo Luis. Mi hermano menor no sabe mucho de ropa. Yo sí sé. A mí me encanta la ropa de moda. Esta tarde voy con él a comprar un traje para la fiesta del viernes. Yo sé de trajes porque me pongo uno todos los días. Puedo recomendarle un almacén. Además, le puedo decir a él qué traje le queda bien y qué traje le queda mal.

ESCUCHAR B, ACTIVIDAD 1

Level 2 Workbook p. 111

WB CD 2, Track 7

Escucha a Carolina. Luego, lee las oraciones y ordénalas según cuándo pasaron. El 1 es lo que pasó primero.

Carolina: Hola, me llamo Carolina. Mi amiga Inés y yo salimos de compras ayer. Primero, fuimos a la tienda de ropa. Inés se compró un suéter muy bonito. Después, fuimos a la zapatería y yo me compré unas sandalias negras que quedan muy bien con mi falda azul. Luego, pasamos dos horas en una joyería. Casi de noche, fuimos a la farmacia. Compramos unos jabones buenos para la cara.

ESCUCHAR B, ACTIVIDAD 2

Level 2 Workbook p. 111

WB CD 2, Track 8

Contesta las siguientes preguntas con oraciones completas.

Inés: Hola, me llamo Inés. Ayer fui de compras. No encontré las botas que siempre tengo ganas de comprar, pero me compré un suéter rojo que queda muy bien con mi falda negra. El viernes es el cumpleaños de mi hermano y voy a dar una fiesta para él. Me parece que me voy a poner el suéter nuevo para la fiesta. A mí me encanta darle regalos a mi hermano porque él es muy bueno conmigo. Ayer, compré un reloj para él.

ESCUCHAR C, ACTIVIDAD 1

Level 2 Workbook p. 112

WB CD 2, Track 9

Escucha a Leonor y toma notas. Luego, coloca en la columna de la izquierda las cosas que compró ella. En la columna de la derecha coloca las cosas que compró su amiga.

Leonor: Hola, soy Leonor y hoy hago las compras de fin de mes. ¡Me encanta ir de compras! Mi amiga Diana viene conmigo y a mí me gusta mucho salir con ella. Hoy fuimos a la tienda de ropa y ella compró una falda negra, un suéter azul y un chaleco gris. Yo compré una falda de cuadros, un cinturón y un abrigo muy lindo. Después, fuimos a la zapatería. Ella compró unas sandalias y yo compré unas botas altas muy de moda.

Audio Scripts

ESCUCHAR C, ACTIVIDAD 2

Level 2 Workbook p. 112

WB CD 2, Track 10

Escucha a Diana y toma notas. Luego, contesta las preguntas.

Diana: Buenas tardes, me llamo Diana. ¡Estoy muy cansada! Salí de compras todo el día. Compré muchas cosas, ¡pero ya todo está cerrado y no puedo comprar más! A mí me encanta comprar ropa, pero no me importa vestirme con ropa de moda. Para mí, es más importante comprar ropa que me queda bien. A mi amiga Leonor sí le gusta la ropa que está de moda. A ella no le interesa cómo le queda. Yo siempre le digo a ella que es más importante buscar la talla y los colores correctos, pero a ella no le importa y tal vez tiene razón: casi nada le queda mal. ¡Qué suerte tiene!

ASSESSMENT SCRIPTS
TEST CD 1

LESSON 1 TEST: ESCUCHAR ACTIVIDAD A

Modified Assessment Book p. 83

On-level Assessment Book p. 114

Pre-AP Assessment Book p. 83

TEST CD 1, Track 15

Escucha el siguiente audio. Luego, completa la actividad A.

Pedro: Oye, Tere, ¿puedes ir conmigo al centro? Esta noche voy a ir al cumpleaños de Ana, mi nueva amiga, y necesito comprar ropa que está de moda. Creo que a Ana le va a gustar.

Tere: Está bien, pero en mi opinión, la ropa no es todo.

Pedro: ¿Qué almacén me recomiendas?

Tere: Te recomiendo el almacén La Nueva Moda. Está cerca de la Librería Cervantes. ¿Qué piensas comprar?

Pedro: Una camisa de rayas, unos pantalones azules y un chaleco.

Tere: Es buena idea. Las rayas están de moda. Vamos.

ACTIVIDAD B

Modified Assessment Book p. 83

On-level Assessment Book p. 114

Pre-AP Assessment Book p. 83

TEST CD 1, Track 16

Escucha el siguiente audio. Luego, completa la actividad B.

Pedro: Tere, ¿cómo me queda esta camisa de rayas? ¿Te gusta?

Tere: Me encanta, pero te queda apretada. ¿Qué talla es?

Pedro: Es talla catorce.

Tere: Entonces necesitas la talla quince.

Pedro: Bien, y los pantalones azules, ¿cómo me quedan? ¿Qué piensas?

Tere: Me parecen muy bonitos y te quedan muy bien. ¡Cómpralos!

Pedro: ¿Compro el chaleco de cuadros?

Tere: Creo que es mala idea. Un suéter es mejor. Mira éste.

Pedro: ¡Muy bien! Lo compro.

HERITAGE LEARNERS SCRIPTS
HL CDs 1 & 3

INTEGRACIÓN HABLAR

Level 2 HL Workbook p. 110

HL CD 1, Track 17

Escucha el mensaje que Victoria dejó en el contestador de su amiga Rita. Toma notas y luego completa la actividad.

FUENTE 2

HL CD 1, Track 18

Rita, te llamo porque estoy muy apurada. Este sábado es la boda de mi hermana y con la dieta y todo el ejercicio que he hecho recientemente estoy más delgada. Fíjate que el vestido me queda mal, me queda muy flojo y se me caen los tirantes de los hombros. ¿Qué hago, Rita? Yo no sé arreglar ropa. Además, mi hermana me dijo que no puedo cambiar el diseño. Llámame.

INTEGRACIÓN ESCRIBIR

Level 2 HL Workbook p. 111

HL CD 1, Track 19

Escucha el mensaje que la señora Corina Veranda, la dueña del almacén, dejó para su esposo Julio en el contestador. Toma notas mientras lo escuchas. Luego realiza la actividad.

FUENTE 2

HL CD 1, Track 20

Julio, te estoy hablando de la oficina de nuestro proveedor. ¿Tienes completo el inventario de este mes? Necesito que me digas qué artículos vendimos más, qué artículos vendimos menos. Dime también, por favor, de cuáles artículos no tenemos más existencias. Creo que voy a pedir cincuenta suéteres rojos porque están muy baratos. ¿Crees que es una buena idea?

LESSON 1 TEST: ESCUCHAR ACTIVIDAD A

HL Assessment Book p. 89

HL CD 3, Track 15

Carla acompaña a Álex a comprarse un traje. Escucha su conversación en la tienda y contesta las preguntas usando oraciones completas.

Álex: Gracias por acompañarme a comprar el traje para la graduación.

Carla: Me encanta hacerlo, Álex. Tú sabes cuánto me gusta ir de compras.

Álex: Será más fácil contigo. Me interesa conocer tu opinión porque tienes buen gusto para la ropa. Siempre sabes cómo combinar los trajes.

Carla: Quiero probarme ese abrigo rojo que está en la vitrina. ¿Me esperas?

Álex: Carla, tengo que comprarlo hoy. Mañana salgo muy tarde del trabajo y las tiendas van a estar cerradas.

Carla: Sólo un minuto. Es justamente lo que buscaba y me va a quedar muy bien con mis botas nuevas.

Álex: Está bien. Voy a ver los trajes mientras tanto.

Carla: No, no. Espera. Quiero tu opinión. ¿Qué te parece?

Álex: Te queda muy bien.

Carla: Sí, y es lo que está de moda.

Álex: ¿Vamos a ver mi traje ahora?

Carla: ¡Claro! Vamos. Ay, mira qué bonita falda de cuadros. Siempre me gusta vestirme a la moda y los cuadros me encantan. ¿Te gusta?

Álex: Sí, sí, pero vamos a ver los trajes, por favor.

Carla: Espera. Es sólo un minuto. ¡Señorita! ¿Tiene esta falda en mi talla?

Álex: Pero, Carla. Creo que…

Carla: Oh, Álex. Este suéter le combina de maravilla. ¡Mira! Y esas sandalias parecen muy cómodas. ¡Me las voy a probar también!

Álex: Pero mi traje, Carla… Yo quisiera…

Audio Scripts

Carla: Hoy tengo suerte y todo lo que veo me gusta y me queda bien…

Álex: Sí. ¡Qué suerte tienes hoy! Creo que voy a volver mañana a comprar mi traje…

Carla: ¡Perfecto, mi amor! Así podemos pasar por la joyería a escoger mi anillo de compromiso.

ACTIVIDAD B

HL Assessment Book p. 89

HL CD 3, Track 16

El tío Mario llegó de Brasil con una gran maleta. Adentro hay regalos para todos. Escucha la conversación y completa luego las partes que faltan.

Mario: ¡Hola! He llegado del Brasil con obsequios para todos.

Raúl: A ver, a ver, ¿qué nos trajiste?

Mario: Primero, un suéter de cuadros para Marina.

Marina: Gracias, tío.

Mario: Enseguida, unas botas rojas para la abuela.

Abuela: ¡Son perfectas! ¿Cómo sabías mi número?

Mario: Y ahora… una pulsera para mamá.

Mamá: ¡Qué linda! Va a combinar con mi falda.

Raúl: ¿Y a mí no me trajiste nada, tío?

Mario: Claro que sí. Te traje un reloj. ¿Te gusta?

Raúl: ¡Me encanta! ¿Tú no te compraste nada, tío?

Tío Mario: Sí, me compré este chaleco que llevo puesto.

UNIDAD 3 Lección 1   Audio Scripts

Audio Scripts

PRESENTACIÓN DE VOCABULARIO

Level 2 Textbook pp. 168–169

TXT CD 4, Track 12

A. Emilio: En el mercado de artesanías muchos de los artículos están hechos a mano. Si quieres comprar artículos de artesanía baratos, puedes regatear por un precio más bajo. Si encuentras algo muy bonito pero muy barato, entonces es una ganga.

B. Emilio: Aquí un señor vende esculturas. Esta escultura es única. No hay otra como ésta.

C. Carolina: Estas joyas son únicas. Son muy finas. Disculpe, ¿me deja ver esas pulseras y aquel collar?

Vendedora: Con mucho gusto, señorita.

Carolina: ¿Me puede decir si están hechos a mano?

Vendedora: Sí, los hice yo. Las pulseras son de plata y el collar es de oro. Son muy finos, ¿no?

Carolina: Sí. Son bellos. Gracias por ayudarme.

Vendedora: De nada.

D. Emilio: Es buena idea ser simpático cuando compras en el mercado…

Carolina: Con permiso, señor. Nos gustaría ver las pinturas.

Vendedor: Pase, señorita. Pase, muchacho. Estamos aquí para ayudarlos.

Emilio: Gracias, señor.

Vendedor: No hay de qué.

¡A RESPONDER!

Level 2 Textbook p. 169

TXT CD 4, Track 13

Escucha las oraciones e indica si son ciertas o falsas según las fotos. Señala con la mano hacia arriba si son ciertas. Señala con la mano hacia abajo si son falsas.

1. Los cinturones son de madera.
2. El collar es de oro.
3. La escultura es un retrato.
4. El retrato es una pintura de una persona.

5. Las artesanías están hechas a mano.
6. Emilio dice «Perdóneme» cuando quiere ver las pinturas.

TELEHISTORIA ESCENA 1

Level 2 Textbook p. 171

TXT CD 4, Track 14

Carolina: ¿Dónde está Emilio? ¡Son las cuatro y media! No podemos empezar porque él tiene la cámara.

Marta: Perdón, señorita, ¿esto está hecho a mano?

Vendedora: Sí, señorita. Es de plata. Y es muy barato.

Marta: ¡Qué bello!

Carolina: Marta, ¿me puedes ayudar, por favor? ¡Puedes ver las artesanías después!

Marta: Esta pintura es muy bella también. ¡Ay, pero qué cara!

Carolina: ¡Marta! ¡Escucha! ¡No tenemos cámara! ¿Qué vamos a hacer ahora?

Marta: Ay, perdón. ¿Qué me preguntaste? Mira, allí viene Emilio.

Emilio: Lo siento. Hace tres horas que camino por toda la ciudad.

Carolina: ¿Y por qué? ¿Para hacer ejercicio?

Emilio: No, para buscar la cámara. La perdí.

ACTIVIDAD 5 - UN REGALO ESPECIAL

Level 2 Textbook p. 174

TXT CD 4, Track 15

Escucha dónde estuvieron Carlitos y su familia durante una excursión. Completa las oraciones para saber qué pasó.

Carlitos: Estuvimos en Ponce, La Perla del Sur, como dicen los ponceños. La idea fue ver las atracciones de la ciudad. No supimos hasta llegar allí que mi mamá también tuvo la idea de comprar artesanías o recuerdos. Estuvimos en el Parque de Bombas primero. Como es un museo, no pude subir a los vehículos. ¡Qué pena! Luego salimos para almorzar. Después del almuerzo fuimos al Museo Castillo Serrallés. Estuvimos en todos los cuartos por dos horas. Luego mi mamá estuvo otra hora en la tienda de artesanías. No pudo salir sin ver las artesanías hechas a mano de madera, de cerámica y de cristal. Puse un recuerdo de un coche de metal rojo en las manos

de mamá y ella lo compró. ¡Por lo menos tuve un recuerdo que me gustó!

TELEHISTORIA ESCENA 2

Level 2 Textbook p. 176

TXT CD 4, Track 16

Emilio: La vi encima de la mesa en casa hoy por la mañana. La puse en mi mochila y salí.

Marta: ¿Y no sabes cuándo la perdiste?

Emilio: No, no sé cuándo la perdí. Lo siento mucho. Primero fui a comprar un regalo de cumpleaños para mi madre: este collar. ¡Es de oro y fue una ganga! Hace un año que pude encontrarla.

Carolina: ¡Emilio! ¡La cámara!

Emilio: ¡Perdón! Estuve un rato en la joyería, después fui a unas tiendas y más tarde comí en un café... Volví al café y a las tiendas, pero no la encontré.

Carolina: ¿Qué estás comiendo?

Emilio: Una galleta de la panadería... ¡La panadería!

PRONUNCIACIÓN

Level 2 Textbook p. 177

TXT CD 4, Track 17

La letra g

Before **a, o, u,** and the consonants **l** and **r,** the Spanish **g** is pronounced like the English g in the word *game.* Listen and repeat.

ga

ganga re**ga**tear ju**ga**r lle**ga**da

go

golf jue**go** ami**go** lue**go**

gu

gusto **gu**apo **Gu**stavo **gu**itarra

gl / gr

globo **Gl**oria **gr**ande **gr**acias

Me **gu**sta ir de compras los domin**go**s para buscar **ga**ngas.

A **Gr**e**go**rio le **gu**sta ju**ga**r al **go**lf.

Audio Scripts

TELEHISTORIA COMPLETA

Level 2 Textbook p. 181

TXT CD 4, Track 18

Escena 1 Resumen

Narrator: Carolina y Marta esperan a Emilio. Por fin llega, pero sin la cámara porque la perdió.

Escena 2 Resumen

Carolina y Marta le preguntan a Emilio dónde está la cámara, pero él no sabe. Cuando ven que Emilio está comiendo una galleta, saben dónde está la cámara: en la panadería.

Escena 3

Marta: ¿Quieres ir al cine mañana?

Álex: Buena idea.

Carolina: Vamos a comenzar...

Marta: Nos vemos mañana, Jeny.

Álex: Hasta luego, mamá.

Carolina: ¿Okay? ¡Acción!

Marta: Con permiso. ¿Me deja ver esa escultura de piedra?

Álex: Con mucho gusto, señorita.

Marta: Es muy fina. ¿Está hecha a mano?

Álex: Sí, yo la hice.

Marta: Entonces, ¿es única?

Álex: Es única, como usted. Yo me llamo Daniel.

Marta: Y yo soy Ariana.

Carolina: ¡Un momento! Marta, Álex, ¿por qué se pusieron esa ropa? ¡Ustedes se vistieron para la segunda parte de la película!

Marta: ¡Ay! ¡Tienes razón! ¡Lo siento!

Álex: Carolina, ¿quieres ir al cine conmigo mañana?

Carolina: Pero... pero, ¿no vas con Marta? ¿Ella no te preguntó...?

Álex: ¿Marta? ¡No! Ella va con Jeny. Me gustaría ir contigo.

Carolina: Entonces, ¡sí!

Álex: ¡Perfecto! Hablamos mañana.

ACTIVIDAD 17 - INTEGRACIÓN

Level 2 Textbook p. 183

TXT CD 4, Track 19

Lee y escucha las descripciones de un mercado. Describe lo que se puede ver y comprar allí, y recomienda a un artesano que quieres visitar.

FUENTE 2

TXT CD 4, Track 20

Listen and take notes.

¿Cuánto tiempo hace que el mercado está allí?

¿Quién es Bety? ¿Qué artículos hace ella?

¿Qué otros artículos puedes encontrar en el mercado?

Announcer: Ahora estamos en el Mercado de la Muralla, un mercado al aire libre donde es posible comprar artesanías hechas a mano. Bety López organiza el mercado.

Bety: Hace cinco años que puse la primera mesa aquí para vender mis animales de cerámica. Después de unos meses, otras personas siguieron mi ejemplo y también pusieron mesas para vender sus artículos.

Announcer: Hoy el mercado es mucho más grande. Aquí puedes encontrar artículos de cuero, joyas de plata y oro, esculturas y mucho más. Si estás en San Juan un sábado, hay que visitarlo. Y... busca a Bety. Siempre está aquí con sus bellos animales de cerámica.

LECTURA CULTURAL: LAS ARTESANÍAS

Level 2 Textbook pp. 184–185

TXT CD 4, Track 21

Hay muchas artesanías típicas de Puerto Rico. Dos muy conocidas son la talla de santos y las «casitas». Las tallas son figuras de madera que representan a los santos de la tradición social puertorriqueña. Primero, el artesano o la artesana trabaja la madera; luego la pinta. Estas tallas llevan símbolos que identifican al santo. Las casitas son fachadas en miniatura de casas y edificios históricos. Existen de muchos tamaños y materiales: las más famosas son de cerámica y son muy finas. Hay también algunas de madera y otras que son básicamente pinturas sobre madera o metal. Las fachadas pueden ser de casas históricas, pero también pueden ser de edificios importantes o de lugares tradicionales, como la de Puig y Abraham, en el Viejo San Juan, que hoy en día es un restaurante muy popular.

En Panamá también hay ricas tradiciones de artesanías. Las molas son una de éstas. Las molas son telas de colores vivos, cortadas y cosidas en diseños del mundo de los cunas. Los cunas, una comunidad indígena de Panamá, hacen estas telas que se conocen internacionalmente. En partes de Panamá también hay artesanos que trabajan la cerámica. Por ejemplo, en el pueblo de La Arena, los artesanos hacen trabajo de cerámica con la arena del lugar. Ellos decoran sus piezas con diseños de la tradición indígena. Las cerámicas de La Arena son únicas.

REPASO: ACTIVIDAD 1 - LISTEN AND UNDERSTAND

Level 2 Textbook p. 188

TXT CD 4, Track 22

Escoge la mejor expresión para responder a la persona.

1. Con permiso. Me gustaría pasar para ver las esculturas sobre la mesa.

2. Gracias por la pulsera. Me gusta mucho.

3. Señora, su retrato es único y muy bonito.

4. Disculpe, ¿me puede decir dónde queda la librería?

5. Le doy quince dólares por el collar de piedra.

6. ¿Ya va a salir?

COMPARACIÓN CULTURAL: ¡ME ENCANTA IR DE COMPRAS!

Level 2 Textbook pp. 190–191

TXT CD 4, Track 23

Perú, Marcos

¡Hola! Soy Marcos. Me encanta comprar regalos para mi familia. Generalmente voy a un centro comercial pero ayer estuve en unas tiendas en la calle. Allí venden artículos de papel, de madera, de cuero y más. Compré un cinturón para mi papá. Después fui a una zapatería y le compré a mi mama unas sandalias de cuero muy de moda. ¡Le encantaron!

Panamá, Juanita

¡Saludos desde Panamá! Mi nombre es Juanita. El sábado pasado fue el cumpleaños de mi hermana mayor.

Audio Scripts

Mi amiga fue conmigo a un mercado al aire libre y ella me ayudó a encontrar una pulsera muy fina de plata. A mi hermana le quedó perfecta. ¡Mi hermana menor mi pidió una también para su cumpleaños!

Puerto Rico, Valeria

¿Qué tal? Me llamo Valeria y vivo en San Juan, Puerto Rico. A veces voy al centro comercial con mis primas o con una amiga. Muchos muchachos y muchachas van allí a pasar el rato. Ayer mi amiga y yo compramos unos sombreros muy bonitos. También compré un vestido, pero me quedó grande. ¡Me encanta comprar ropa!

REPASO INCLUSIVO: ACTIVIDAD 1 LISTEN, UNDERSTAND, AND COMPARE

Level 2 Textbook p. 192

TXT CD 4, Track 24

Listen to this announcement about community events and then answer the following questions.

Buenos días. Aquí estoy yo, Roberto Gómez, para hablar de unas actividades de nuestra comunidad. Si te interesa vestirte con la ropa que está muy de moda y te importa llevar ropa que te queda bien, entonces tienes suerte. Visita el centro comercial Las Palmas este viernes de 10 a 10. Va a abrir una nueva tienda donde puedes encontrar la mejor ropa y también los mejores relojes y pulseras. Si te encantan las gangas, esta tienda es la tienda para ti.

También este sábado va a abrir la nueva panadería Las Delicias en el centro. Compra dos panes por el precio de uno. La panadería está abierta de 7:00 a.m. a 5:00 p.m. y el domingo de 7:00 a 12:00. Está cerrada los domingos por la tarde.

Si tienes un evento especial en la comunidad, llámanos con la información. Gracias por escuchar.

WORKBOOK SCRIPTS
WB CD 2

INTEGRACIÓN HABLAR

Level 2 Workbook p. 131

WB CD 2, Track 11

Escucha el mensaje que le dejó Jorge a su hermana en el celular. Toma apuntes.

FUENTE 2

WB CD 2, Track 12

Jorge: Hola, Carla. Vengo de hacer algunas compras. Compré el regalo de cumpleaños de la abuela y también algunas cosas para ti. A la abuela le compré una pulsera de plata muy bella. Es una joya única y cara, pero pude regatear para un buen precio. Vi muchas joyas bellas para ti, como ahillos de oro y aretes de plata. Preferí los aretes de plata. ¡Sé que te van a gustar! A nuestro hermano Raúl le compré una chaqueta y unos jeans azules. A nuestros padres les compré unas esculturas de metal muy lindas.

INTEGRACIÓN ESCRIBIR

Level 2 Workbook p. 132

WB CD 2, Track 13

Escucha el mensaje que le dejó Fátima a Victoria. Toma apuntes.

FUENTE 2

TXT CD 2, Track 14

Fátima: Hola, Victoria. Yo también fui al mercado de artesanías en Perú. Compré una escultura de metal hecha a mano y una pintura para mi cuarto. Compré unos artículos de cerámica para mi madre y un retrato para mi padre.

También encontré un anillo, una pulsera y un collar de plata. Además, compré ropa hecha a mano para mis hermanos. Todos los regalos fueron caros, pero pude regatear un poco.

ESCUCHAR A, ACTIVIDAD 1

Level 2 Workbook p. 133

WB CD 2, Track 15

Escucha a Carmen. Luego, marca con una cruz las cosas que ella compró.

Carmen: Hace tres semanas que fui al mercado de artesanías. Estuve allí todo el día. Compré una escultura de metal para mi mamá y un retrato de Napoleón para mi papá. También compré un collar de piedras y una pulsera de plata para mí. Mis amigas prefirieron comprar pulseras de oro, pero a mí me gustó más la de plata.

ESCUCHAR A, ACTIVIDAD 2

Level 2 Workbook p. 133

WB CD 2, Track 16

Escucha a Blanca. Luego, contesta las preguntas.

Blanca: Mi hija me dio una bella escultura de cerámica. Hace muchos años que quiero una escultura nueva. Ésta es muy grande —demasiado grande para ponerla en la mesa—. Entonces la puse en el piso, delante de la ventana. ¡Nunca tuve una escultura tan bonita! Fue una sorpresa. Yo no pedí este regalo, pero cuando la vio, mi hija supo que era el regalo perfecto.

ESCUCHAR B, ACTIVIDAD 1

Level 2 Workbook p. 134

WB CD 2, Track 17

Escucha a Norma. Luego, lee las oraciones y contesta **cierto** o **falso**.

Norma: Nada me gusta más que ir al mercado de artesanías. Hace más de cinco años que voy todos los meses. Siempre voy con una amiga a la que también le encanta ir. Hoy por la mañana fuimos las dos. Mi amiga se durmió temprano anoche y así pudo levantarse y llegar a las siete, cuando abre el mercado. Yo no pude llegar tan temprano porque mi casa está lejos y tuve que llevar a mi hija al gimnasio. Pero nosotras nos vimos allí a las ocho, y allí estuvimos todo el día.

Audio Scripts

ESCUCHAR B, ACTIVIDAD 2

Level 2 Workbook p. 134

WB CD 2, Track 18

Escucha a Alicia. Luego, contesta las preguntas.

Alicia: ¡Me encanta el mercado de artesanías! Hoy compré muchas cosas, pero no tuve que pagar demasiado: encontré buenos precios. Es difícil poner precio a un artículo único, hecho a mano. Pero el señor que me vendió una hermosa pulsera de plata le puso un precio bajo. ¡Fue una ganga! Y no tuve que regatear: hace más de siete años que nos conocemos. ¡Es un buen amigo!

ESCUCHAR C, ACTIVIDAD 1

Level 2 Workbook p. 135

WB CD 2, Track 19

Escucha a Ramiro y decide si las siguientes oraciones son ciertas o falsas. Corrige las falsas.

Ramiro: Yo hago artesanías. Hace más de treinta años que trabajo en el mercado de artesanías de la ciudad vieja. Aprendí primero a hacer esculturas de madera; mi padre me enseñó. Pero después supe también cómo hacer artículos de cuero, como sandalias, chalecos, abrigos y cinturones. Hace dos años que mi hija empezó a ayudarme en la tienda. Ella ya pudo aprender todo. ¡Un día lo va a hacer todo mejor que yo!

ESCUCHAR C, ACTIVIDAD 2

Level 2 Workbook p. 135

WB CD 2, Track 20

Escucha el diálogo entre Ramiro y un cliente. Luego, contesta las preguntas con oraciones completas.

Cliente: Buenos días, señor… disculpe, ¿puedo hablar con usted?

Ramiro: Sí, señorita. Pase. ¿De qué me quiere hablar?

Cliente: Es que… ayer estuve aquí, y… me puse esta gorra de cuero que usted hizo. Estuve aquí por un rato viendo cosas y después salí…

Ramiro: …salió con la gorra.

Cliente: Sí, ¡perdóneme! Lo supe cuando llegué a casa y no tuve tiempo para volver. Aquí le doy el dinero. ¿Son 20 dólares?

Ramiro: Sí, gracias.

Cliente: No, señor, gracias a usted.

Ramiro: ¡No hay de qué!

ASSESSMENT SCRIPTS
LESSON 2 TEST: ESCUCHAR ACTIVIDAD A

Modified Assessment Book p. 95

On-level Assessment Book p. 131

Pre-AP Assessment Book p. 95

TEST CD 1, Track 17

Escucha el siguiente audio. Luego, completa la actividad A.

Buenos días, señoritas. Miren todo lo que tengo aquí a precios muy baratos. Todos mis artículos están hechos a mano. Estas pulseras de plata son una ganga. Sólo cuestan quince dólares. Las hice yo. Muy bonitas, ¿verdad? Este collar es de oro. Es muy fino. Cuesta treinta y cinco dólares. ¿Lo compran? Las esculturas son de madera, también hechas a mano. Las hizo mi papá. Son muy bonitas. Éstas aquí son de metal. Las de madera cuestan ocho dólares y las de metal cuestan veinte dólares. Entonces, ¿qué artículo me van a comprar?

ACTIVIDAD B

Modified Assessment Book p. 95

On-level Assessment Book p. 131

Pre-AP Assessment Book p. 95

TEST CD 1, Track 18

Escucha el siguiente audio. Luego, completa la actividad B.

Inés: Las esculturas son muy bonitas, pero no me interesan. ¿Me deja ver ese collar de oro?

Vendedor: Con mucho gusto.

Inés: Me gusta mucho. Le doy veinte dólares.

Vendedor: Lo siento, señorita. No puedo. ¿Qué le parecen treinta dólares? Es una ganga.

Inés: No, para mí es mucho dinero. ¿En cuánto me da esta pulsera de plata?

Vendedor: ¿Qué le parecen trece dólares?

Inés: No, le doy diez dólares.

Vendedor: Doce dólares.

Inés: Está bien. Aquí tiene usted.

Vendedor: Gracias, señorita.

Inés: De nada. Adiós.

UNIT 3 TEST: ESCUCHAR ACTIVIDAD A

Modified Assessment Book p. 107

On-level Assessment Book p. 143

Pre-AP Assessment Book p. 107

TEST CD 1, Track 19

Escucha el siguiente audio. Luego, completa la actividad A.

Inés: ¿Me deja ver esa pulsera de plata, por favor?

Vendedora: Con mucho gusto. Es muy fina, ¿no?

Inés: Me encanta. Es para mi mamá. ¿Cuánto cuesta?

Vendedora: Veinticinco dólares, pero se la dejo en veinte dólares. Es una ganga.

Inés: Muy bien. La compro. ¿Cuánto cuesta esta escultura de madera?

Vendedora: Está hecha a mano. Una cuesta quince dólares, pero le vendo dos por veinticinco dólares.

Inés: Me parece que es un buen precio. Son para mi papá. También las compro.

Vendedora: ¿Qué le parecen estas sandalias de cuero? Se las doy por doce dólares. Muy baratas.

Inés: Son perfectas para mi hermana. Gracias.

Vendedora: No hay de qué. Hoy usted hizo buenas compras conmigo.

Inés: Creo que sí. Y no tuve que regatear. Adiós.

ACTIVIDAD B

Modified Assessment Book p. 107

On-level Assessment Book p. 143

Pre-AP Assessment Book p. 107

TEST CD 1, Track 20

Escucha el siguiente audio. Luego, completa la actividad B.

Pedro: Buenos días. ¿Me deja ver estos zapatos en negro, número ocho, por favor?

Vendedor: Con mucho gusto. Espere un momento. Aquí los tiene usted.

Pedro: Me quedan apretados. Creo que necesito el número nueve.

Audio Scripts

Vendedor: Pronto vuelvo. Lo siento, pero sólo tengo el número nueve en marrón.

Pedro: Bueno, me los voy a poner. A ver... Éstos sí me quedan bien. Los compro.

HERITAGE LEARNER SCRIPTS
HL CDs 1 & 3

INTEGRACIÓN HABLAR

Level 2 HL Workbook p. 133

HL CD 1, Track 21

Escucha el mensaje que dejó Enrique López a su amigo Rico. Toma notas y luego completa la actividad.

FUENTE 2

HL CD 1, Track 22

Rico, te llamo para decirte que me inscribí en la clase de pintura de la escuela de manualidades. Empiezo este sábado al mediodía. La primera clase la da la pintora famosa Verónica Huerta, la que nos visitó la semana pasada en la escuela, ¿te acuerdas? Pagué $45 dólares por cuatro sesiones pero creo que valen la pena. Ah, se me olvidaba... Mi hermana Rosa va a tomar la clase de papel maché. ¿En cuál te vas a inscribir tú? Llámame cuando tengas tiempo.

INTEGRACIÓN ESCRIBIR

Level 2 HL Workbook p. 134

HL CD 1, Track 23

Escucha el recado que Jorge Silva dejó para su esposa Sonia. Toma apuntes y completa la actividad.

FUENTE 2

HL CD 1, Track 24

Sonia, acabamos de aterrizar en el aeropuerto. Tengo muchas ganas de verte. Traigo varios regalos para ti y para nuestros hijos. A Joaquín le traje un cinturón hecho de cuero. A la abuela Beatriz le compré las tazas y los platos de cerámica que me pidió. Los encontré en un mercado de artesanías en San Juan. El precio original de la vajilla era de $200 dólares pero después de regatear, la vendedora me la vendió a $65. ¿Puedes creerlo? A Marisela le compré una pulsera de oro y a ti te traje la escultura de Gutier

Martín, tu artesano favorito. Bueno, ya tenemos que bajarnos del avión, te veo en un rato.

LESSON 2 TEST: ESCUCHAR
ACTIVIDAD A

HL Assessment Book p. 101

HL CD 3, Track 17

Roberto y Miguel van a comprar un regalo para su amiga Silvia. Escucha su conversación y contesta las preguntas usando oraciones completas.

Miguel: ¿Sabes que mañana es el cumpleaños de Silvia?

Roberto: Oh, sí. Lo había olvidado. ¿Tienes un regalo para ella?

Miguel: No. Precisamente quiero proponerte que le compremos uno.

Roberto: ¿Tienes idea de qué le puede gustar?

Miguel: Sí. Ya he pensado en algo. Creo que no va a ser muy difícil.

Roberto: Confío en tu buen gusto. Vamos.

Miguel: Esta tienda es nueva. Vamos a ver aquí.

Roberto: Buenas tardes. ¿Podemos ver lo que tienen en la tienda?

Vendedor: Por supuesto. Pasen, por favor.

Miguel: Gracias. ¿Nos deja ver el departamento de artesanías?

Vendedor: Con mucho gusto. Es por aquí. Tenemos artículos de diferentes materiales: madera, piedra, cuero...

Roberto: ¿Crees que a Silvia le gusta la artesanía?

Miguel: Seguro. El año pasado la acompañé a una exposición de artesanía latinoamericana y la escuché hablar de cuánto le gusta.

Roberto: No lo sabía. A mí también me gusta.

Miguel: Mira esta figura de cerámica. ¡Es hermosa!

Vendedor: Tiene incrustaciones de metal y está pintada a mano.

Roberto: Creo que le gustará.

Vendedor: Es una pieza única, muy fina, de un artesano mexicano.

Miguel: ¿No será muy cara?

Vendedor: Es bastante barata para lo exquisita que es. Son sólo $50.00

Miguel: Si la pagamos entre los dos...

Roberto: Es una verdadera ganga. La llevaremos.

Vendedor: ¿Desean que la envuelva para regalo?

Miguel: Sí, por favor.

Roberto: Muchas gracias.

Vendedor: No hay de qué. Con permiso. Enseguida vuelvo.

Miguel: Seguro que Silvia va a estar feliz con este regalo.

Roberto: Yo también lo estaría.

ACTIVIDAD B

HL Assessment Book p. 101

HL CD 3, Track 18

Escucha el diálogo y luego completa los parlamentos que faltan.

Clienta: Perdí dos de botones de mi blusa. ¿Tendrá unos iguales?

Vendedora: Déjeme ver... No, no tengo botones iguales a ésos.

Clienta: Tal vez tenga unos parecidos.

Vendedora: Sí, tal vez... Déjeme buscar un poco más. ¿Qué tal éstos?

Clienta: No, son más grandes que los míos. No pasarán por el ojal.

Vendedora: ¿Éstos tal vez? Se parecen bastante.

Clienta: El color es muy intenso, se nota mucho la diferencia.

Vendedora: Tendré que buscar más. ¡Hay tantos modelos!

Clienta: Yo veré en esta caja mientras usted mira en la otra.

Vendedora: Con mucho gusto.

Clienta: ¿Sabe qué? Mejor cambio todos los botones.

Vendedora: No es mala idea. Y los nuevos son bonitos.

UNIT 3 TEST: ESCUCHAR
ACTIVIDAD A

HL Assessment Book p. 113

HL CD 3, Track 19

Un grupo de amigos está de compras antes de regresar a casa. Escucha la conversación que sostienen y responde a las preguntas usando oraciones completas.

Carla: Esta tienda es nueva. Vamos a ver aquí.

Vendedor: Buenas tardes, ¿puedo ayudarlos con algo?

Audio Scripts

Miguel: Gracias. Estamos buscando algo especial para llevar a casa.

Vendedor: ¿Les gustaría ver el departamento de artesanías? Tenemos artículos en arcilla, madera, piedra, cuero…

Miguel: ¿Será que a la abuela le gusta algo de artesanía?

Carla: Seguro. El año pasado la acompañé a una exposición de artesanía maya y me dijo cuánto le gusta.

Miguel: No lo sabía. A mí también me gusta.

Carla: ¡Mira estas casitas! ¡Son hermosas!

Vendedor: Están hechas de arena pintada con detalles en madera y hojas.

Miguel: Creo que ésta le gustará.

Vendedor: Es una pieza típica de nuestros indígenas.

Miguel: Muy bien. La llevamos.

Vendedor: ¿Desean que se las envuelva para regalo?

Miguel: Sí, por favor.

Carla: Muchas gracias.

Vendedor: No hay de qué. Con permiso. Enseguida vuelvo.

Miguel: ¿Dónde estarán Tomás y Cristina? Hace un par de horas que se fueron.

Carla: Allá vienen, cargados de bolsas.

Tomás: ¡No van a creer las cosas que conseguimos para los chicos!

Cristina: Entramos a esta tienda fabulosa que está del otro lado del centro comercial.

Carla: ¿Y qué tanto compraron?

Tomás: Conseguimos la flauta de bambú para Pedro.

Carla: ¡Qué bueno! ¡Va a estar encantado!

Miguel: Y esos caracoles, ¿para quién son?

Tomás: Uno es para ti, Carla, y el otro es para mamá.

Carla: ¡Gracias, hermano! Sabes que me gustan mucho los caracoles.

ACTIVIDAD B

HL Assessment Book p. 113

HL CD 3, Track 20

Escucha al narrador del programa de radio y responde a las siguientes preguntas. Usa oraciones completas para dar tus respuestas.

Anunciador: Buenas tardes, amigos de la música caribeña. Nuestro programa de hoy está dedicado a la música de Puerto Rico.

La música puertorriqueña es el resultado de la fusión de ritmos propios como la **décima**, **seis**, música **folklórica**, la **danza**, la **plena**, la **bomba** y la **salsa**, y de otros ritmos importados como el **son** y el **mambo** de Cuba, el **merengue** de la República Dominicana, el **jazz** de los Estados Unidos y el **bolero**.

Puerto Rico, con su inmenso mundo musical, ha dado muchos músicos excelentes al crisol melódico de América Central y del Caribe. Entre ellos se encuentra Rafael Hernández Marín, cuyas letras de canciones son un espejo del sentir y vivir del pueblo puertorriqueño.

Las obras de Rafael Hernández, uno de los compositores más importantes de la música puertorriqueña durante el siglo 20, han logrado desafiar las pruebas del tiempo. Su herencia al pueblo consta de más de 3,000 composiciones musicales de diversos géneros, incluyendo clásicos tales como: «Silencio», «Ausencia», «Campanitas de Cristal», «Preciosa», «El Cumbanchero» y «Lamento Borincano».

Este gran músico y compositor nació en Aguadilla, Puerto Rico, el 24 de octubre de 1892 y murió en su Viejo San Juan el 11 de diciembre de 1965.

UNIDAD 3 Lección 2 Audio Scripts

Map/Culture Activities *Puerto Rico*

1 Además de la isla principal (*main*) de Puerto Rico, hay dos islas más que forman parte del país: Culebra y Vieques. Localízalas y escribe sus nombres en el mapa.

2 Puerto Rico tiene costa con dos océanos o mares distintos. Identifícalos y escribe sus nombres en el mapa.

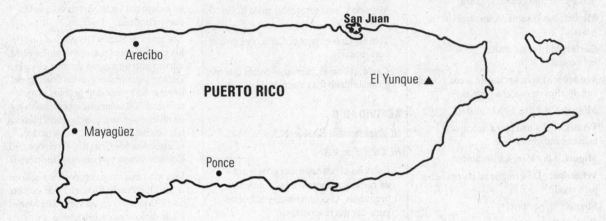

3 ¿Cómo se llama el país hispanohablante (*Spanish-speaking country*) al oeste (*west*) de Puerto Rico?

UNIDAD 3

Map/Culture Activities

84

Unidad 3
Map/Culture Activities

¡Avancemos! 2
Unit Resource Book

Map/Culture Activities *Puerto Rico*

4 Usa la información de la página 140 de tu libro para elegir la respuesta correcta que completa las frases a continuación.

1. Benicio del Toro es famoso por el trabajo que hace en el mundo del _____ .

    a. cine   **b.** fútbol   **c.** baile

2. El ingrediente principal de los tostones son _____ .

    a. frijoles   **b.** bananas   **c.** arroz

3. La bandera de Puerto Rico comparte los colores con la bandera de _____ .

    a. Estados Unidos   **b.** México   **c.** Bolivia

4. Vieques es una _____ hermosa de Puerto Rico.

    a. ciudad   **b.** montaña   **c.** isla

5 Los puertorriqueños son conocidos también como **boricuas**, una palabra indígena de los taínos, la gente nativa de la isla. ¿Se usan palabras indígenas para nombrar a personas, ciudades o animales donde vives? Menciona algunas de ellas y di cuál es su origen étnico.

_____

_____

_____

6 ¿Para qué construyeron (*built*) «el Morro» los españoles? ¿Hay edificios o estructuras similares donde tú vives? ¿Para qué fueron construidos (*were they built*)?

_____

_____

_____

UNIDAD 3 Map/Culture Activities

Map/Culture Activities Answer Key

PUERTO RICO

❶ See map below.

❷ See map below.

❸ República Dominicana

❹
1. a
2. b
3. a
4. c

❺ *Answers will vary.*

❻ *Answers will vary.*

UNIDAD 3

Map/Culture Activities
Answer Key

Fine Art Activities

El Gobernador don Miguel Antonio de Ustáriz, José Campeche

Puerto Rican artist José Campeche is considered one of the most important painters of the eighteenth century Americas. His interest in the arts originated with his father, also a painter, and led to his training with the official painter of the Spanish court. This painting of Puerto Rican governor Miguel Antonio de Ustáriz is one of Campeche's best-known portraits. It is a good example of the Rococo style popular at the time. This style focused on carefree, delicate, and graceful depictions of the aristocracy.

Complete the activities below based on your observations of *El Gobernador don Miguel Antonio de Ustáriz*, by José Campeche.

1. Many portrait artists of the time included key images or colors in their paintings to symbolize the specific qualities or achievements of their subjects. Explain the traits or accomplishments of the governor that Campeche symbolizes by including the following features in his painting:

   a. The color gold _____

   b. The sword at the governor's side _____

   c. The city map in the governor's hand _____

   d. The architectural plan sliding off the table _____

2. If you were commissioned to paint the portrait of a significant political or cultural figure from our time, whom would you choose? What visual details would you include to give the public clues about his or her personality and achievements?

   _____
   _____
   _____
   _____
   _____
   _____

El Gobernador don Miguel Antonio de Ustáriz (1792), José Campeche. Oil on wood. Instituto de Cultura Puertorriqueña, San Juan, Puerto Rico.

Fine Art Activities

Bisonte con palmeras (Bison with Palm Trees), Goyena Family (19th century)

The Goyena family were important contributors to the Puerto Rican art tradition. The heads of the Goyena family were Joaquín Goyena and Ysabel M. O'Daly. Joaquín was an artist who painted in miniature, and his works are detail-oriented. He married Ysabel, who was born in Galway, Ireland. Ysabel played a key role in the development of Puerto Rican artists who worked before the independence of the island.

Study *Bisonte con palmeras* from the Goyena Family, and answer the questions below.

1. What details can you see in the painting?

   _____

   _____

   _____

   _____

2. How does a miniature painting compare to a regular-sized painting? In other words, How would this work be different if it were painted on a large scale?

   _____

   _____

   _____

   _____

   _____

   _____

   _____

Bisonte con palmeras (Bison with Palm Trees) (ca. 1825–1850), Goyena Family. Watercolor on ivory, 2 3/8 x 2 in. (6.1 x 5.2 cm). Teodoro Vidal Collection (1996.91.16), Smithsonian American Art Museum, Washington, DC/Art Resource, NY.

UNIDAD 3 Lección 1

Fine Art Activities

Fine Art Activities

La fiesta del vejigante, Obed Gómez

Although Puerto Rican painter Obed Gómez showed remarkable artistic talent from the age of three, he resisted becoming a professional painter for almost thirty years. He currently works and lives in Florida, but his subject matter is inspired primarily by the culture and spirit of his homeland. His paintings are characteristically executed in bright pastels and acrylics. *La fiesta del vejigante* depicts a traditional celebration in the town of Loiza. During the feast of Santiago Apóstol, **los vejigantes** parade down the streets in masks and colorful, flowing costumes.

Discuss your interpretation of *La fiesta del vejigante*, by Obed Gómez, in the following activities.

1. Focus on the colors used in the painting to answer the following questions.

   a. What do you think the mood of the painting is? How do the colors in *La fiesta del vejigante* create mood?

   _____

   _____

   b. How does Gómez use color to create effects of light, shadow, and depth? Use examples from the painting in your answer.

   _____

   _____

   _____

2. What do you think this celebration might commemorate? Write a short response about the possible origins of this holiday.

   _____

   _____

   _____

   _____

La fiesta del vejigante (2005), Obed Gómez. Acrylic on canvas, 30″ x 40″. Courtesy of the artist.

Fine Art Activities

Descenso del paraíso, Edward Ferraioli

Artist Edward Ferraioli studied design in both the United States and his native Puerto Rico. He has experience in marble engraving, jewelry making, and both metalwork and glasswork. Recently Ferraioli has gained recognition for his decorative glass mosaics. A mosaic is an ancient art form in which very small pieces of glass, stone, or tile are set into wet plaster to create carefully detailed images.

1. What images from nature do you see in the mosaic?

    _____

    _____

2. How does the artist use the images and color to create the illusion of downward movement?

    _____

    _____

    _____

    _____

    _____

Descenso del paraíso (2002), Edward Ferraioli. Mosaico en cristal sobre madera, 39″ x 96″. Courtesy of Instituto de Cultura Puertorriqueña, San Juan, Puerto Rico.

Fine Art Activities Answer Key

EL GOBERNADOR DON MIGUEL ANTONIO DE USTÁRIZ, JOSÉ CAMPECHE, *p. 87*

1. *Answers will vary. Answers given are possible suggestions:*
   a. high position in society
   b. strength, fortitude
   c. he holds the city in his hands
   d. progress

2. *Answers will vary.* Students should name their subject, location, and visual details of the portrait, etc.

BISONTE CON PALMERAS (BISON WITH PALM TREES), GOYENA FAMILY (19TH CENTURY), *p. 88*

1. *Answers will vary. Possible answers:* The mountains, sky, and water in the background are close in color. The two palm trees intertwine a bit and their trunks are multicolored. The ground is bumpy and the artist portrays the bison's muscles.

2. *Answers will vary. Possible answer:* The large-scale painting will require the viewer to step back, while the miniature painting will ask the viewer to step toward the painting. The proximity to the painting will change the relationship between the viewer and the paintings. The viewer will have to make an effort to relate to a smaller painting, while a big painting suggests that the viewer is part of the experience.

LA FIESTA DEL VEJIGANTE, OBED GÓMEZ, *p. 89*

1a. *Answers will vary.*
   b. *Answers will vary.* Students may note that color is used in place of traditional light/dark shading.
2. *Answers will vary.*

DESCENSO DEL PARAÍSO, EDWARD FERRAIOLI, *p. 90*

1. *Answers will vary.* The mosaic includes a plant stem, leaves, and flower petals. It is most likely a depiction of a cascading Bird of Paradise, a plant native to Puerto Rico and the Caribbean.

2. *Answers will vary.* The flower petals point downwards, the eye follows the central line of the plant from top to bottom, the yellow specks become more diffused and the darker blue draws focus to the lower half of the mosaic.

UNIDAD 3 Fine Art Activities Answer Key

Date: _____

Dear Family:

We are about to begin *Unidad 3*, of the Level 2 *¡Avancemos!* program. It focuses on authentic culture and real-life communication using Spanish in Puerto Rico. It practices reading, writing, listening, and speaking, and introduces students to culture typical of Puerto Rico.

Through completing the activities, students will employ critical thinking skills as they compare the Spanish language and the culture of Puerto Rico with their own community. They will also connect to other academic subjects, using their knowledge of Spanish to access new information. In this unit, students are learning to talk about clothing, shopping, personal needs, past activities and events, and items at a marketplace. They are also learning to say whom things are for, to express themselves courteously, and to express opinions. They are also learning about grammar—verbs like **gustar,** the present tense of irregular **yo** verbs, pronouns after prepositions, **hace** + expressions of time, preterite of **-ir** stem-changing verbs, and irregular preterite verbs.

Please feel free to call me with any questions or concerns you might have as your student practices reading, writing, listening, and speaking in Spanish.

Sincerely,

Family Involvement Activities

coat – el abrigo   *boots* – las botas   *vest* – el chaleco   *dress* – el vestido   *shirt* – la camisa

belt – el cinturón   *skirt* – la falda   *watch* – el reloj   *suit* – el traje   *T-shirt* – la camiseta

bracelet – la pulsera   *cap* – la gorra   *sandals* – las sandalias   *shoes* – los zapatos   *pants* – los pantalones

STEP 1

Draw each of the above items on a small piece of cardboard or an index card. Make two copies for each item, and write the name of the item in Spanish underneath the picture (you will have a total of thirty cards).

STEP 2

Shuffle the cards and place them face down on a table. Invite your family to play. Each player takes a turn flipping over two cards. Each time a card is flipped over, the player reads the word under the drawing in Spanish.

STEP 3

If you make a match (flip over two identical cards), keep the pair and go again. If the images do not match, replace them face down and let the next player go. The aim of the game is to match as many pairs as possible and to practice the words you learned in this unit. The person who gathers the most pairs wins.

Keep track of which player collects the most pairs per round.

Absent Student Copymasters

Presentación / Práctica de vocabulario

Materials Checklist

☐ Student text

☐ DVD 1

☐ Video Activities Copymasters, pages 50 and 51

☐ *Cuaderno,* pages 99–101

☐ *Cuaderno para hispanohablantes,* pages 99–102

☐ TXT CD 4 Tracks 1–2

☐ Did You Get It? Copymasters, pages 1–2

☐ ClassZone.com

Steps to Follow

☐ Study the vocabulary of **Presentación de vocabulario** (pp. 144–145) by looking at the photos and reading the words and accompanying text. Watch the DVD and complete the Video Activities Copymasters.

☐ Listen to TXT CD 4 Track 1 as you read the vocabulary words again. Repeat the words aloud after you hear them.

☐ Practice the words of the **Más vocabulario** box on page 145. Read the words aloud. Write the words in your notebook.

☐ Do **Práctica de vocabulario** (p. 146). Complete **Actividades 1**, **2**, and **3**.

☐ Complete *Cuaderno,* pages 99, 100, and 101.
OR
Complete *Cuaderno para hispanohablantes,* pages 99, 100, 101, and 102.

☐ Check your comprehension by completing the **Para y piensa** box on page 146.

☐ Complete Did You Get It? Copymasters, pages 1 and 2.

If You Don't Understand . . .

☐ Watch the DVD in a quiet place. If you get lost, stop the DVD and go back.

☐ Listen to the CD as many times as you need to complete the activity.

☐ Reread the directions for the activity you find difficult. Write the directions in your own words.

☐ Use the Interactive Flashcards to help you study the lesson.

Absent Student Copymasters

Vocabulario en contexto

Materials Checklist

- [ ] Student text
- [ ] DVD 1
- [ ] Video Activities Copymasters, pages 52 and 53
- [ ] TXT CD 4 Track 3
- [ ] Did You Get It? Copymasters, pages 1 and 3

Steps to Follow

- [ ] Look at the photos on page 147. What do you think is happening?
- [ ] Read **Cuando lees** and **Cuando escuchas** under *Strategies* (p. 147). Copy the questions.
- [ ] Complete **Cuando lees** before watching the DVD.
- [ ] Watch the DVD for **Unidad 3**, **Telehistoria escena 1** without your book. Then watch the DVD again and complete the Video Activities Copymasters.
- [ ] Look at the dialogue in the book. Follow along in the book as you listen to TXT CD 4 Track 3. Use the pictures and context to help you understand the dialogue.
- [ ] Complete **Actividades 4** and **5** on page 148.
- [ ] Check your comprehension by completing the **Para y piensa** box on page 148.
- [ ] Complete Did You Get It? Copymasters 1 and 3.

If You Don't Understand . . .

- [ ] Use the images to help you understand the DVD.
- [ ] Listen to the CD in a quiet place. If you get lost, stop the CD and go back.
- [ ] Review the activity directions and study the model. Try to follow the model in your own answers.
- [ ] If you have any questions, write them down so you can ask your teacher later.
- [ ] Practice both parts of any partner activities.
- [ ] Think about what you are trying to say when you write a sentence. After you write your sentence, check to make sure that it says what you wanted to say.

Absent Student Copymasters

Presentación / Práctica de gramática

Materials Checklist

- [ ] Student text
- [ ] *Cuaderno,* pages 102–104
- [ ] *Cuaderno para hispanohablantes,* pages 103–105
- [ ] TXT CD 4 Track 4
- [ ] Did You Get It? Copymasters 4, 5, 11
- [ ] ClassZone.com

Steps to Follow

- [ ] Study the present tense of irregular **yo** verbs (p. 149).
- [ ] Do **Actividades 6**, **7**, **8**, and **9** (pp. 150–151).
- [ ] Complete *Cuaderno,* pages 102, 103, and 104.
  OR
  Complete *Cuaderno para hispanohablantes,* pages 103, 104, and 105.
- [ ] Check your comprehension by completing the **Para y piensa** box on page 151.
- [ ] Complete Did You Get It? Copymasters 4, 5, and 11.

If You Don't Understand . . .

- [ ] For activities that require listening, listen to the CD in a quiet place. If you get lost, stop the CD and go back.
- [ ] Do the activities you understand first.
- [ ] Read the model a few times so you are certain that you understand what to do. Follow the model.
- [ ] Read everything aloud. Be sure that you understand what you are reading.
- [ ] If you have any questions, write them down for your teacher.
- [ ] Read your answers aloud to make sure they say what you wanted to say.
- [ ] Use the Animated Grammar to help you understand.
- [ ] Use the Leveled Grammar Practice on the @Home Tutor.

Absent Student Copymasters

Gramática en contexto

Materials Checklist

- [ ] Student text
- [ ] DVD 1
- [ ] Video Activities Copymasters, pages 54 and 55
- [ ] TXT CD 4 Track 5
- [ ] Did You Get It? Copymasters 4, 6, 10

Steps to Follow

- [ ] Look at the photo on page 152. What do you think is happening?
- [ ] Read **Cuando lees** and **Cuando escuchas** under *Strategies* (p. 152). Copy the questions.
- [ ] Read the script and try to understand the dialogue based on the picture. Try to answer the question in **Cuando lees**.
- [ ] Watch the DVD for **Unidad 3**, **Telehistoria escena 2** without your book. Then watch the DVD again and complete the Video Activities Copymasters.
- [ ] Look at the dialogue in the book. Follow along in the book as you listen to TXT CD 4 Track 5. Use the pictures and context to help you understand the dialogue.
- [ ] Study the words in the **También se dice** box.
- [ ] Complete **Actividades 10**, **11**, and **12** on page 153.
- [ ] Check your comprehension by completing the **Para y piensa** box on page 153.
- [ ] Complete Did You Get It? Copymasters 4, 6, and 10.

If You Don't Understand . . .

- [ ] Make sure you are in an area where you can concentrate.
- [ ] Reread the activity directions. Write the directions in your own words.
- [ ] Write the model on your paper. Try to follow the model in your own answers.
- [ ] Read aloud everything that you write. Be sure that you understand what you are reading.
- [ ] Write down any questions you have for your teacher.
- [ ] If you need a partner to complete the activity, do both parts of the activity.
- [ ] Think about what you are trying to say when you write a sentence. After you write your sentence, check to make sure that it says what you wanted to say.

Absent Student Copymasters

Presentación / Práctica de gramática

Materials Checklist

☐ Student text

☐ *Cuaderno,* pages 105–107

☐ *Cuaderno para hispanohablantes,* pages 106–109

☐ TXT CD 4 Track 6

☐ Did You Get It? Copymasters 7–8

☐ ClassZone.com

Steps to Follow

☐ Study pronouns after prepositions (p. 154).

☐ Do **Actividades 13** and **14** (p. 155).

☐ Listen to TXT CD 4 Track 6 as you follow along in the **Pronunciación** activity on page 155.

☐ Do **Actividades 15** and **16** (p. 156).

☐ Complete *Cuaderno,* pages 105, 106, and 107.
OR
Complete *Cuaderno para hispanohablantes,* pages 106, 107, 108, and 109.

☐ Check your comprehension by completing the **Para y piensa** box on page 156.

☐ Complete Did You Get It? Copymasters 7 and 8.

If You Don't Understand . . .

☐ Listen to the CD as many times as you need to complete the activity.

☐ Review the section before completing the activities.

☐ Read the model a few times so you are certain that you understand what to do. Follow the model.

☐ Say what you want to write before you write it.

☐ If you have any questions, write them down for your teacher.

☐ If you need a partner to complete the activity, practice both parts instead.

☐ Read your answers aloud to make sure they say what you wanted to say.

☐ Use the Animated Grammar to help you understand.

☐ Use the Leveled Grammar Practice on the @Home Tutor.

Absent Student Copymasters

Todo junto

Materials Checklist

- [ ] Student text
- [ ] DVD 1
- [ ] Video Activities Copymasters, pages 56 and 57
- [ ] *Cuaderno,* pages 108–109
- [ ] *Cuaderno para hispanohablantes,* pages 110–111
- [ ] TXT CD 4 Tracks 7–9
- [ ] WB CD 2 Tracks 1–4
- [ ] HL CD 1 Tracks 17–20
- [ ] Did You Get It? Copymasters 7, 9

Steps to Follow

- [ ] Look at the photos on page 157. What do you think is happening?
- [ ] Read **Cuando lees** and **Cuando escuchas** under *Strategies* (p. 157). Copy the questions.
- [ ] Review the content of **Unidad 3, Telehistoria escena 1** and **escena 2**.
- [ ] Read the script and try to understand the dialogue based on the picture. Try to answer the questions in **Cuando lees**.
- [ ] Watch the DVD for **Unidad 3, Telehistoria escena 3** without your book. Then watch the DVD again and complete the Video Activities Copymasters.
- [ ] Look at the dialogue in the book. Follow along as you listen to TXT CD 4 Track 7. Use the pictures and context to help you understand the dialogue.
- [ ] Complete **Actividades 17, 18, 19, 20,** and **21** on pages 158 and 159.
- [ ] Complete *Cuaderno,* pages 108 and 109.
  OR
  Complete *Cuaderno para hispanohablantes,* pages 110 and 111.
- [ ] Check your comprehension by completing the **Para y piensa** box on page 159.
- [ ] Complete Did You Get It? Copymasters 7 and 9.

If You Don't Understand . . .

- [ ] Make sure you can watch the DVD in a quiet place.
- [ ] Listen to the CD in a quiet place. If you get lost, stop the CD and go back.

UNIDAD 3 Lección 1

Absent Student Copymasters

Absent Student Copymasters

Lectura y Conexiones

Materials Checklist

☐ Student text

☐ TXT CD 4 Track 10

Steps to Follow

☐ Read **¡Avanza!** and *Strategy*: **Leer** (p. 160).

☐ Read **Revista de moda** on pages 160 and 161.

☐ Look at the drawings and reread the article.

☐ Follow along with the text on TXT CD 4 Track 10.

☐ Check your comprehension by completing the **¿Comprendiste?** and **¿Y tú?** sections of the **Para y piensa** box on page 161.

☐ Read **Los taínos** on page 162.

☐ Read **Proyecto 1**, **El lenguaje**. Try to find some words of taíno origin.

☐ Read **Proyecto 2**, **La geografía**. Do the research as directed.

☐ Read **La música** in **Proyecto 3**. Try to find a CD of salsa music and identify the instruments. Answer the questions in the exercise.

If You Don't Understand . . .

☐ Listen to the CD in a quiet place. Listen as many times as necessary.

☐ Read everything aloud. Be sure that you understand what you are reading.

☐ Say what you want to write before you write it.

☐ If you have any questions, write them down so you can ask your teacher later.

☐ After you write a sentence, check to make sure that it says what you wanted to say.

Absent Student Copymasters

Repaso de la lección

Materials Checklist

☐ Student text

☐ *Cuaderno,* pages 110–121

☐ *Cuaderno para hispanohablantes,* pages 112–121

☐ TXT CD 4 Track 11

☐ WB CD 2 Tracks 5–10

Steps to Follow

☐ Read the bullet points under **¡Llegada!** on page 164.

☐ Complete **Actividades 1**, **2**, **3**, **4**, and **5** (pp. 164–165).

☐ Complete *Cuaderno,* pages 110, 111, and 112.

☐ Complete *Cuaderno,* pages 113, 114, and 115.
OR
Complete *Cuaderno para hispanohablantes,* pages 112, 113, 114, and 115.

☐ Complete *Cuaderno,* pages 116, 117, and 118.
OR
Complete *Cuaderno para hispanohablantes,* pages 116, 117, and 118.

☐ Complete *Cuaderno,* pages 119, 120, and 121.
OR
Complete *Cuaderno para hispanohablantes,* pages 119, 120, and 121.

If You Don't Understand . . .

☐ Make sure you are in an area where you can concentrate.

☐ Reread the directions for the activity you find difficult. Write the directions in your own words.

☐ If you are having trouble with an activity, complete the ones you can do first.

☐ Write the model on your paper. Try to follow the model in your own answers.

☐ If you have any questions, write them down for your teacher to answer later.

☐ Think about what you are trying to say when you write a sentence. After you write your sentence, check to make sure that it says what you wanted to say.

Absent Student Copymasters

Presentación / Práctica de vocabulario

Materials Checklist

☐ Student text

☐ DVD 1

☐ Video Activities Copymasters, pages 58 and 59

☐ TXT CD 4 Tracks 12–13

☐ *Cuaderno,* pages 122–124

☐ *Cuaderno para hispanohablantes,* pages 122–125

☐ Did You Get It? Copymasters 12–13

☐ ClassZone.com

Steps to Follow

☐ Study the vocabulary of **Presentación de vocabulario** (pp. 168–169) by looking at the photos and reading the words and accompanying text. Watch the DVD and complete the Video Activities Copymasters.

☐ Read the vocabulary words again as you listen to TXT CD 4 Track 12. Repeat the words aloud after you hear them.

☐ Practice the words of the **Más vocabulario** box on page 169. Read the words aloud. Write the words in your notebook.

☐ Do **Práctica de vocabulario** (p. 170). Complete **Actividades 1** and **2**.

☐ Complete *Cuaderno,* pages 122, 123, and 124.
OR
Complete *Cuaderno para hispanohablantes,* pages 122, 123, 124, and 125.

☐ Check your comprehension by completing the **Para y piensa** box on page 170.

☐ Complete Did You Get It? Copymasters 12 and 13.

If You Don't Understand . . .

☐ Watch the DVD in a quiet place. If you get lost, stop the DVD and go back.

☐ Listen to the CD in a quiet place. If you get lost, stop the CD and go back.

☐ Practice both parts of any partner activities.

☐ Use the Interactive Flashcards to help you study the lesson.

Absent Student Copymasters

Vocabulario en contexto

Materials Checklist

☐ Student text

☐ DVD 1

☐ Video Activities Copymasters, pages 60 and 61

☐ TXT CD 4 Track 14

☐ Did You Get It? Copymasters 12, 14

Steps to Follow

☐ Look at the photos on page 171. What do you think is happening?

☐ Read **Cuando lees** and **Cuando escuchas** under *Strategies* (p. 171). Copy the questions.

☐ Try to answer the question in **Cuando lees** before watching the DVD.

☐ Watch the DVD for **Unidad 3**, **Telehistoria escena 1** without your book. Then watch the DVD again and complete the Video Activities Copymasters.

☐ Look at the dialogue in the book. Follow along in the book as you listen to TXT CD 4 Track 14. Use the pictures and context to help you understand the dialogue.

☐ Complete **Actividades 3** and **4** on page 172.

☐ Check your comprehension by completing the **Para y piensa** box on page 172.

☐ Complete Did You Get It? Copymasters 12 and 14.

If You Don't Understand . . .

☐ Use the images to help you understand the DVD.

☐ Listen to the CD in a quiet place. If you get lost, stop the CD and go back.

☐ Do the activities you understand first.

☐ Read the model before starting so you know what to do. Follow the model.

☐ Say what you want to write before you write it.

☐ Write down any questions you have for your teacher.

☐ If you need a partner to complete the activity, practice both parts instead.

☐ After you write a sentence, check to make sure that it says what you wanted to say.

Absent Student Copymasters

Presentación / Práctica de gramática

Materials Checklist

☐ Student text

☐ *Cuaderno,* pages 125–127

☐ *Cuaderno para hispanohablantes,* pages 126–128

☐ TXT CD 4 Track 15

☐ Did You Get It? Copymasters 15, 16, 21

☐ ClassZone.com

Steps to Follow

☐ Study irregular preterites (p. 173).

☐ Do **Actividades 5**, **6**, **7**, and **8** (pp. 174–175).

☐ Complete *Cuaderno,* pages 125, 126, and 127.
OR
Complete *Cuaderno para hispanohablantes,* pages 126, 127, and 128.

☐ Check your comprehension by completing the **Para y piensa** box on page 175.

☐ Complete Did You Get It? Copymasters 15, 16, and 21.

If You Don't Understand . . .

☐ For activities that require listening, listen to the CD in a quiet place. If you get lost, stop the CD and go back.

☐ Do the activities you understand first.

☐ Reread the activity directions. Write the directions in your own words.

☐ Write the model on your paper. Try to follow the model in your own answers.

☐ If you have any questions, write them down for your teacher.

☐ Practice both parts of any partner activities.

☐ Read your answers aloud to make sure they say what you wanted to say.

☐ Use the Animated Grammar to help you understand.

☐ Use the Leveled Grammar Practice on the @Home Tutor.

Absent Student Copymasters

Gramática en contexto

Materials Checklist

- [ ] Student text
- [ ] DVD 1
- [ ] Video Activities Copymasters, pages 62 and 63
- [ ] TXT CD 4 Tracks 16–17
- [ ] Did You Get It? Copymasters 15, 17

Steps to Follow

- [ ] Look at the photo on page 176. What do you think is happening?
- [ ] Read **Cuando lees** and **Cuando escuchas** under *Strategies* (p. 176). Copy the questions.
- [ ] Read the script and try to understand the dialogue based on the picture. Try to answer the questions in **Cuando lees**.
- [ ] Watch the DVD for **Unidad 3**, **Telehistoria escena 2** without your book. Then watch the DVD again and complete the Video Activities Copymasters.
- [ ] Look at the dialogue in the book. Follow along in the book as you listen to TXT CD 4 Track 16. Use the pictures and context to help you understand the dialogue.
- [ ] Complete **Actividades 9** and **10** on page 177.
- [ ] Listen to TXT CD 4 Track 17 as you follow along in the **Pronunciación** activity on page 177.
- [ ] Check your comprehension by completing the **Para y piensa** box on page 177.
- [ ] Complete Did You Get It? Copymasters 15 and 17.

If You Don't Understand . . .

- [ ] Make sure you are in an area where you can concentrate.
- [ ] Review the section before completing the activities.
- [ ] Read the model a few times so you are certain that you understand what to do. Follow the model.
- [ ] Read everything aloud. Be sure that you understand what you are reading.
- [ ] Write down any questions you have for your teacher.
- [ ] If you need a partner to complete the activity, do both parts of the activity instead.

Absent Student Copymasters

Presentación / Práctica de gramática

Materials Checklist

☐ Student text

☐ *Cuaderno,* pages 128–130

☐ *Cuaderno para hispanohablantes,* pages 129–132

☐ Did You Get It? Copymasters 18, 19, 22

☐ ClassZone.com

Steps to Follow

☐ Study the preterite of **-ir** stem-changing verbs (p. 178).

☐ Do **Actividades 11**, **12**, and **13** (pp. 179–180).

☐ Complete *Cuaderno,* pages 128, 129, and 130.
OR
Complete *Cuaderno para hispanohablantes,* pages 129, 130, 131, and 132.

☐ Check your comprehension by completing the **Para y piensa** box on page 180.

☐ Complete Did You Get It? Copymasters 18, 19, and 22.

If You Don't Understand . . .

☐ Review the activity directions and study the model. Try to follow the model in your own answers.

☐ Say what you want to write before you write it.

☐ If you have any questions, write them down for your teacher.

☐ Read your answers aloud to make sure they say what you wanted to say.

☐ Use the Animated Grammar to help you understand.

☐ Use the Leveled Grammar Practice on the @Home Tutor.

Absent Student Copymasters

Todo junto

Materials Checklist

- [ ] Student text
- [ ] DVD 1
- [ ] Video Activities Copymasters, pages 64 and 65
- [ ] *Cuaderno,* pages 131–132
- [ ] *Cuaderno para hispanohablantes,* pages 133–134
- [ ] TXT CD 4 Tracks 18–20
- [ ] WB CD 2 Tracks 11–14
- [ ] HL CD 1 Tracks 21–24
- [ ] Did You Get It? Copymasters 18, 20

Steps to Follow

- [ ] Look at the photos on page 181. What do you think is happening?
- [ ] Read **Cuando lees** and **Cuando escuchas** under *Strategies* (p. 181). Copy the questions.
- [ ] Review the content of **Unidad 3**, **Telehistoria escena 1** and **escena 2**.
- [ ] Read the script and try to understand the dialogue based on the picture. Try to answer the questions in **Cuando lees**.
- [ ] Watch the DVD for **Unidad 3**, **Telehistoria escena 3** without your book. Then watch the DVD again and complete the Video Activities Copymasters.
- [ ] Look at the dialogue in the book. Follow along as you listen to TXT CD 4 Track 18. Use the pictures and context to help you understand the dialogue.
- [ ] Complete **Actividades 14**, **15**, **16**, **17**, and **18** on pages 182 and 183.
- [ ] Complete *Cuaderno,* pages 131 and 132.
  OR
  Complete *Cuaderno para hispanohablantes,* pages 133 and 134.
- [ ] Check your comprehension by completing the **Para y piensa** box on page 183.
- [ ] Complete Did You Get It? Copymasters 18 and 20.

If You Don't Understand . . .

- [ ] Watch the DVD in a quiet place. If you get lost, stop the DVD and go back.
- [ ] Listen to the CD as many times as you need to complete the activity.

Absent Student Copymasters

Lectura cultural

Materials Checklist

☐ Student text

☐ TXT CD 4 Track 21

Steps to Follow

☐ Read *Strategy* (p. 184).

☐ Read **Las artesanías** on pages 184 and 185.

☐ Look at the photos and reread the text.

☐ Follow along with the text on TXT CD 4 Track 21.

☐ Check your comprehension by completing the **¿Comprendiste?** and **¿Y tú?** sections of the **Para y piensa** box on page 185.

If You Don't Understand . . .

☐ Make sure you are in an area where you can concentrate.

☐ Listen to the CD as many times as necessary.

☐ Read everything aloud. Be sure that you understand what you are reading.

☐ Write down any questions you have for your teacher.

☐ Think about what you are trying to say when you write a sentence. After you write your sentence, check to make sure that it says what you wanted to say.

Absent Student Copymasters

Proyectos culturales

Materials Checklist

☐ Student text

Steps to Follow

☐ Read the text of **Comparación cultural** and look at the illustrations (p. 186).

☐ Read the description of **Una máscara moderna** in **Proyecto 1**. Try to make one of your own.

☐ Read the description of **Una máscara antigua** in **Proyecto 2**. Try to make one of your own.

☐ Read the **En tu comunidad** segment, and write your answer in your notebook.

If You Don't Understand . . .

☐ Read the activity directions a few times, silently and then aloud.

☐ If you have any doubts or observations, write them down so you can discuss them with your teacher later.

Absent Student Copymasters

Repaso de la lección

Materials Checklist

☐ Student text

☐ *Cuaderno,* pages 133–144

☐ *Cuaderno para hispanohablantes,* pages 135–144

☐ TXT CD 4 Track 22

☐ WB CD 2 Tracks 15–20

Steps to Follow

☐ Read the bullet points under **¡Llegada!** on page 188.

☐ Complete **Actividades 1**, **2**, **3**, **4**, and **5** (pp. 188–190).

☐ Complete *Cuaderno,* pages 133, 134, and 135.

☐ Complete *Cuaderno,* pages 136, 137, and 138.
OR
Complete *Cuaderno para hispanohablantes,* pages 135, 136, 137, and 138.

☐ Complete *Cuaderno,* pages 139, 140, and 141.
OR
Complete *Cuaderno para hispanohablantes,* pages 139, 140, and 141.

☐ Complete *Cuaderno,* pages 142, 143, and 144.
OR
Complete *Cuaderno para hispanohablantes,* pages 142, 143, and 144.

If You Don't Understand . . .

☐ Listen to the CD as many times as you need to complete the activity.

☐ Reread the activity directions for the activity you find difficult. Write the directions in your own words.

☐ Write the model on your paper. Try to follow the model in your own answers.

☐ If you have any questions, write them down for your teacher to answer later.

☐ Read your answers aloud to make sure they say what you wanted to say.

Absent Student Copymasters

Comparación cultural

Materials Checklist

☐ Student text

☐ *Cuaderno,* pages 145–147

☐ *Cuaderno para hispanohablantes,* pages 145–147

☐ TXT CD 4 Track 23

Steps to Follow

☐ Read the directions in **Lectura y escritura** for **Actividades 1** and **2** on page 190.

☐ Listen to TXT CD 4 Track 23 as you read **¡Me encanta ir de compras!** in the text (pp. 190–191).

☐ Read the strategy for **Escribir**, then begin **Actividad 2**.

☐ Complete the **Compara con tu mundo** section on page 190.

☐ Complete *Cuaderno,* pages 145, 146, and 147.
OR
Complete *Cuaderno para hispanohablantes,* pages 145, 146, and 147.

If You Don't Understand . . .

☐ Look over all the instructions for **Leer** and **Escribir** before you begin to read the feature again.

☐ Listen to the CD in a quiet place. Pause and go back as often as necessary. Repeat unfamiliar words aloud.

☐ Look up words you don't know. Keep a list of new vocabulary.

☐ If you get confused, make a list of questions to ask your teacher later.

☐ Think about what you want to say before you begin writing. Reread everything you write. Check for punctuation, spelling, and verb–subject agreement.

Absent Student Copymasters

UNIDAD 3 Lección 2

Absent Student Copymasters

Repaso inclusivo

Materials Checklist

☐ Student text

☐ TXT CD 4 Track 24

Steps to Follow

☐ Use TXT CD 4 Track 24 to complete **Actividad 1** on page 192. Imitate the voices on the CD.

☐ Complete **Actividades 2**, **3**, **4**, **5**, **6**, and **7** (pp. 192–193).

If You Don't Understand . . .

☐ For **Actividad 1**, listen to the CD in a quiet place. If you get lost, pause the CD and go back.

☐ Use the textbook and review the vocabulary and verb conjugations you need to complete each activity.

☐ Write and practice the parts of all participants in activities that call for partner or group work.

☐ Think about what you want to say before you begin to write. Make sure that it makes sense. Read aloud everything that you write.

☐ If you have any questions, write them down for your teacher to answer later.